TRICKED

My Life as a Child Sex Trafficking Survivor

Mary Mau with Mary StJohn-Putnam

Copyright © 2024 by Mary Frances Mau

All rights reserved.

No portion of this book may be reproduced in any form without written permission from the publisher or author, except as permitted by U.S. copyright law.

Author's Note

When I started writing this book, just before my 50th birthday, I'd lived and worked in Waikiki for more than thirty years, and was still in the life—the sex trade. I could make all the money I wanted because, even though I was middle aged and a grandma, I could still turn heads and cause traffic accidents. I worked out hard, didn't do any drugs or even drink, and I'd had 20-plus surgeries (thanks body dysmorphia!). I looked like porno Barbie. The money, jewels, nice car, and attention—all the exterior glamor—felt like sunshine and rainbows. But inside, another story.

I knew I had to make a change, but had no idea how, lacked self-esteem, and didn't know who to trust. Over the years, I've seen and helped many young girls who showed up on the street, and I hoped that sharing my story and secrets for survival might help these girls get out. Or at least live to share their own stories. I scribbled a few paragraphs and mentioned my vision to a retired Honolulu Police Department officer, who knew a professional writer. Little by little, I trusted more people who could help me reach an even bigger audience.

I'm not writing this because I want your sympathy. That's the farthest thing from what I want. I hope that when you see how I survived and made it out of the life and onto something good, you'll believe that it's possible for anyone to make huge changes in their life.

I'm also not in it for the money. Material things matter little to me anymore. I tend to give away things, like my stuff and my heart.

Even though I've made millions over the years, I never got good at saving much. Except my daughter and, eventually, myself.

Thank you for your interest in my story and the broader story of human trafficking. With your help, I hope we can save many others.

Some names have been changed to protect the not-so innocent.

A portion of the proceeds from this book will go to helping combat human trafficking here in the U.S. and around the world.

Chapter One

Four Fathers, But Only One Mommy

I was the middle child of five, born in 1960 from the third father of four fathers. My mother had my older sister with a Canadian, my older brother with a Danish guy, me with a Middle Eastern American, and my two little sisters with an Italian—like the International House of Fathers! My brother, sisters and I had four fathers. But we just had one mother. And not for very long.

One horrible morning in 1974, I woke up shivering in the house we had only been in for a few months. It was on the other side of Buffalo from our old house so I had to get up extra early to catch three different buses to get to my elementary school. Up in the attic my mom still had all the extra boxes unopened from two moves ago. Boxes that traveled around with us, some marked, "fancy gadgets" or "Stan's stuff." All Stan the Jerk's crap.

We kept his stuff because Mommy thought, she didn't want to admit it though, that Stan the Jerk might come back from Vegas someday and say he was sorry for slugging her in the gut and calling her a whore. She would smile and surprise him by presenting him with all his boxes. He would think it was romantic and everything would be back to how it was before.

Life with Stan had not been that great. I didn't understand why Mom liked him so much. Right before he left, he'd wrapped a phone cord around her neck, stabbed her with an ice pick, and lit all her clothes on fire. Did she think this meant love? Some kind of weird form of passion? I also didn't understand how her latest, Carter, didn't seem to mind the way Mommy went on about her ex Stan right in front of him.

Mom and Carter weren't actually married, but lately Carter was the only adult paying attention. I hoped he wouldn't leave. Carter and Mom both drank and smoked too much, trying to forget the ex and all their troubles. They'd end up arguing and calling each other nasty names.

Only Carter and I got up early, me with all the buses to catch, and Carter with whatever he did all day. Mostly helping my mom with me and my two younger sisters. So mornings were nice and quiet. I could imagine the day would bring new wonders to my life. Or at least a good pick-up hockey game. Morning was also the only time I was allowed to eat Captain Crunch. It wasn't the real kind, we couldn't afford the brand-names. But I'd gotten pretty good at pretending our stuff was just as good as other people's.

I stood by the kitchen heater shivering, soaking up the warmth. The heater made me feel comfy and sleepy and I didn't want to move away. Carter came down the stairs in worn-out boxer shorts and a Black Sabbath t-shirt. I had a quilt wrapped around me with pajamas and slippers and he was barefoot, not noticing the cold. I asked him once how come he was never cold and he told me, "When you're friends with Johnny Walker Red, you're never cold or alone."

He had half-moon bags under his eyes. He went right to the table to his Marlboro red-box cigarettes I'd walked down to the corner Bodega to buy for him the day before. He sat down and lit one up, sparking a horrible coughing jag. Sounded like his innards might come up through this mouth. His red face bloated, eyes bulged.

He drank and smoked like Stan the Jerk, but that's where the similarities ended. He loved Mom and took care of her. They'd argue, but he never hit like Stan.

"Loopie," Carter said, "Would you be a doll and make me a cup of Sanka?" He always called me Loopie. Like the boxes in the garage, the nickname was from a previous dad, the only one I ever thought of as my *real* dad, Bert. I used to crawl around in my crib, in a circle, like a dog does before it lies down. I crawled in a loop so Bert called me Loopie and it stuck.

I hustled over, already moving in that direction, and put the pot on to boil. While we waited, I took down a bowl, got out a spoon and went to the cupboard for the box of fake Captain Crunch. When I pulled it down, I realized there was hardly any left.

My day was ruined.

I poured what was left and added milk to let it sit. I liked the cereal softened by the milk before I ate it, so it wouldn't be too sharp and scrape the roof of my mouth.

The whole time I didn't look at Carter. I didn't want him to tell me how Mom's mood was last night. Two long weeks ago she'd stopped going to the bar, missing her barmaid shifts because she was sick. We lived mostly on Mom's tips, the reason the groceries were thinning out. The fake Captain Crunch was first to go. Mom had not showered and changed clothes since the day her mood turned so dark. It scared me, scared me more than anything else in the world, and there was nothing I could do about it.

She wouldn't talk to me. She wouldn't talk to anyone. I didn't know what was wrong. I told her I was sorry I stayed out late over at the hockey park. I told her I was sorry for not doing the laundry or the dishes when I should have. It didn't help.

Just a few weeks before, Carter caught her with a razor in the bath. She'd made a little cut on her wrist. Carter got mad and yelled at her. Mommy broke her silence and screamed that he didn't understand her. No one understood her and she couldn't take it anymore. Carter went around the house, picked up the scissors, all the kitchen knives and anything else with a sharp edge.

I sat down at the table, the cigarette smoke hanging in the air. Normally I would've gone into the living room to get away from it but I needed to be close to someone this morning, even if it was only Mom's latest boyfriend. I didn't want to like him, not too much since I didn't know how long he would last.

He drank his Sanka and puffed. "It was real bad last night, Loopie. I know you don't want to hear it, but I think we need to take her in. She needs to get professional help."

I spooned some yellow mush into my mouth. Tears burned my eyes. The cereal tasted bland. I nodded. Mommy would be put in a county hospital, a horrible place with no doors or windows. No pictures on the walls. No color anywhere.

Carter reached over and put his hand on mine. I pulled my hand away. He looked a little hurt.

He said, "You better get ready for school." He got up, the hand with the cigarette held onto the table for balance as he tipped back his cup and drank the rest of the Sanka. He walked out and up the stairs.

I pushed the bowl away without eating the last of the Captain Crunch.

From up at the top of the stairs Carter screamed, "Loopie!"

He never screamed. I had a bad feeling about this and I stood with shaky knees. All the world narrowed to that staircase.

He yelled again, "Loopie, get up here. Loopie." His voice cracked.

I walked without feeling the steps. Carter stood in the doorway to Mommy's room, his face all scrunched up. I had never seen him cry. He stepped back.

Mommy lay on the bed, naked, empty pill bottles all around. Her milky blue eyes stared at the ceiling. She was all gray. I sucked in a breath, not sure I could breathe again.

I didn't have a good idea of time. It seemed to stretch out and slow down and get fuzzy in parts. I remember I didn't have to take all those buses that morning. I was pretty sure I wasn't supposed to see what I saw there in Mommy's bedroom.

An ambulance came with a guy wearing a shirt that said CORONER in big letters across the back. He kept trying to keep me out of the room. He smelled like a hospital, but had kind eyes.

Somehow I had this idea that if I just went back there and looked at her one more time, I would see her blink. I looked in again, and again, hoping it would be like *The Wizard of Oz* and it was all just a dream and everything would be back to normal.

The world swirled around. People moved in and out. I sat on the couch in the living room and stared at the dark TV. No one bothered to turn on. My little half-Italian sisters were curled up on either side of me, asleep, finally, after they cried themselves out. My own tears did not want to come. People came in and out and said things you say when you don't know what to say. I stared at the blackness of the screen, seeing blurred reflections of people moving in and out of the room. If I were the lady in *Bewitched* I could wiggle my nose and change everything. Could I bring someone back to life? Once Mommy and Stan had gotten into a fight over which show was better, *Bewitched* or *I Dream of Jeannie*. At least, that's what their words said, but somehow the fight felt like it was about something else.

Like magic, the bad kind of magic from an evil witch, Stan came back from Vegas. Like a tornado.

I tried to stay out of the way, head down. But I couldn't get the image stuck in my head, of Mommy's milky blue eyes. I tried to focus on Carter, his hair disheveled, his face shaggy with a beard, his eyes blood red. Then both men were there in the kitchen at the same time. Was that the day after she died? Time was muddled and people were, too: these two men of Mommy's that shouldn't have been in the same place at the same time. Carter looked at my face, then came and sat down next to me at the kitchen table. It seemed like forever since that awful morning, at this very same table, before life turned into a nightmare. Before they took Mommy away.

I was glad to have something familiar and close to me, even though it was just Carter. I could almost feel something.

Stan didn't even slow down. I don't remember him saying any words. He stared down Carter then kept moving through the house, moving the furniture out.

Carter took up my hand. He looked at me with sad eyes. "We'll be alright, Loopie, it'll all be okay." His face looked like he meant it, but didn't quite believe it. Like he needed to convince himself more than me.

Carter feared Stan like everyone else in the neighborhood. His drunken violent episodes where Stan beat man or wall, whichever came into view first. Word whispered around had him deeply involved in the Mafia, quick with a gun or switchblade. Stan had heard these stories and did nothing to dispel the allegations of Mafia ties or violent tendencies. The jerk liked the power and fame. His being away caused the image and rumors to grow.

He moved through our house like he owned it, everything in it, and the whole entire world.

Carter said, "He just wants the furniture. And that damn safe of your mother's. Said he paid cold hard cash for it. Said he'd take the little girls, too."

He let that hang in the air, watching me closely. Which girls? My little sisters? Not me. Even if he wanted me I did *not* want to go with him. He was crazy. He lived far away. He was not *my* dad.

Carter looked at me harder, then away. "He talked about your sisters like," his voice trailed off, or maybe I just didn't want to hear, "like they were furniture, too." I didn't know if I wanted to be like furniture, hauled off. I wanted to be wanted, didn't I? But not like furniture. Who would want me? Who would take care of me?

"He really just wants the safe," I muttered. I don't think I was supposed to know about that either. "He's scared of what's in it."

"What are you talking about? There's something in the safe he wants? I've seen the safe, there's nothing in it, no money."

"She didn't tell you?" I couldn't say Mommy or even her given name. The way I felt I didn't think I ever would be able to say it again.

"It's why he never came back. She said if he didn't come back to her she was going to give them to the police. But he never came back."

Carter looked at me like I was a grown up. "What's 'them'?"

"She never gave up the books. He called her bluff." That's the way Mommy used to say it. She lost the card game with the shitty hand God dealt her. Would these little things she used to say keep popping up in my head all the time?

"And now he wants them so no one else will see them and give them to the police."

"What? What are you talking about?" Carter glanced toward the ceiling. We could hear more furniture being dragged across the floor.

"She kept these little composition books like we have for school, and wrote down everything Stan the Jerk ever did or bragged that he did. Poems and stuff too. He wants those books."

Carter stood. He waited a moment. "We can't let him have them." Again, like he was trying to convince himself.

He looked at the front door, anxious, ready to flee. I didn't blame him. He'd already stayed longer than I thought he would. "Do you know the combination?"

I shook my head.

"Then there's nothing we can do."

My Nana stormed into the kitchen and stared at Carter.

"What are you saying to this poor girl!" Her arms swallowed me in a warm, safe hug. I loved her more than anybody. Even Mommy. That was a bad thing to think. I loved Mommy too. Right?

She swept me up and away. Carter yelled as we left.

"We can't let him have that. It isn't fair," Carter yelled. Mad at the world. Mad that this ex was stomping all over his life and home. "That jerk had money, lots of money and never gave any to her or to his girls."

Nana shouted over her shoulder. "That's not Loopie's concern, she's just a little girl."

Carter wasn't listening. He shouted to no one or everyone, mad at the world. "That asshole left his family to fend for themselves!"

The woman he loved, my mother, had treated Carter like dirt. Then left us all alone. We didn't know what to do without so much as a word from her—didn't people write notes when they did this? He told me the only thing she'd said the night before was, "Take care of my babies," and he thought she just meant to make sure we got to bed with our teeth brushed that night. He didn't realize until too late she meant: *when I'm gone.*

I didn't see the explosion when Stan blew up the safe. I vaguely recall a loud sound off in the distance, as I stared at the ceiling from the sofa at Nana's house. I didn't know what the sound was at the time. I remember thinking *thunder* or *bomb* but there was no rain, and no war like in the movies.

Later when Nana brought me back to the house to get some clothes, I saw the ruined black box on the charred front lawn. The neighbors said he used dynamite. A few ashes still hung in the fading light of the day. Suspended in the dusk. They got all blurry as tears swelled at the bottom part of my eyes. The ashes went soft and fuzzy, not yet ready to fall to the ground.

Chapter Two

North via Nana's

My mom's best friend who became a bonus mom—I called her Nana— already had a ton of kids to worry about. Still, Nana spent extra time with me while the male grown-ups decided my fate. She liked these paint-by-numbers kits from the dime store down the street, and sat at the table in her kitchen, "Where the light is good," she'd say. Her canvas had sections, each with a number printed in it that went with a mini bucket of paint. These buckets, connected like paper dolls holding hands, were only the size of her thumb. She'd look closely at the picture on the cover of the kit before starting.

The week my mom died, I got to skip all those buses to get to my sixth-grade class. Nana had a kit of a girl wearing a floppy yellow hat with a ribbon around it. After Nana had a good look, I stared at the picture too, trying to decide if the girl was smiling or not. Her perfect red lips seemed to be turned up slightly on the sides, like a smile, but something in her large gray-blue eyes looked sad. Had she lost someone, too?

Nana looked at all the choices of colors, and picked up one of the rows of connected paints. I liked the smell of a freshly cracked open mini-bucket. It smelled new, like art was about to happen. She pulled open the plastic top on the light skin-color that made up the biggest part of the girl's face. Her perfectly oval button nose took up three sections with a couple more sections for shading around it.

"Good to start with the light colors," she told me.

"Why?" A favorite word back then.

"Because if you accidentally get some of the light colors in the dark, you can't really tell. Like if it bleeds over," she explained patiently. "But if you get the dark colors mixed in with the light, they get all muddy-looking."

That was true, too, with my crayons. If I got yellow in the wrong section I could color over it with black or brown, but not the other way around. "It's like coloring for grown-ups." I said.

She smiled and chuckled, and patted me on the head. "Yeah, you're right." She looked me right in the eye. "You're so smart."

Nana told me so many things like this when I was young. And it's not that I didn't believe her, because I knew she was wise like Glinda, the Good Witch of the South. I knew that Nana knew things, I just wasn't yet smart enough to believe everything she said to me, deep in my heart. It would take years of me learning things for myself, learning things the hard way, to realize how much she knew, and how my life might've been easier if I'd listened to her sooner.

She only had a couple of brushes, one for the lighter colors and one for the darker ones. Like doing the laundry. Lights in this pile. Darks in the other. She dipped the light brush into that peachy skin-colored bucket, and dabbed at the girl's cheek, so careful, so gentle, like it was a real girl whose face she'd just touched with her brush.

She'd asked me if I wanted my own kit to work on with her. "No," I'd said. "I like watching you do it." Her hands were so delicate, holding the brush just so, like she could've been her own painting—"My Nana in the Kitchen Doing Paint-by-Numbers."

Painting let Nana escape her chaos, the mess left by all the kids she cared for, the husband who needed her. Here she could have some kind of order. Something beautiful but simple. She could be somewhere else, some*one* else for a while. An artist.

I didn't want to be anywhere else but next to her. That's not what was decided, in spite of my kicking and screaming and trying really hard not to cry.

Stan the Jerk packed up our house and took away my younger sisters. My older siblings, barely old enough to take care of themselves, couldn't take me. I was sent to Newfoundland, Canada, to live with relatives I barely knew. My first time on an airplane.

I figured the stewardesses were extra nice to me because I was a kid. One other kid got on the plane before everyone else, in front of me. Even though his mother was barely taller than me, hardly strong enough to carry his sad whiny self, she lugged him on the plane. Part of me wanted someone to carry me, too. Hold me close.

He looked over her shoulder and stuck out his tongue at me. I was tempted to stick out my tongue back at him, but a bigger part of me wanted to not be a kid anymore. I wanted to be grown up and not need anyone to give me special attention on a plane, or have anyone to tell me where I would live. I wanted to be grown up because grownups get to decide what to do with their lives all on their own.

Still, I watched, hoping I wasn't turning green with envy, as the mom got her son buckled in, and then said a tearful goodbye. He didn't make a sound until she was out of his sight, and then he screamed his head off. I wanted to turn to him and tell him, "That's nothing, *you're* going to see her again. *Your* mommy is still *alive* at least."

Then it hit me, I might see my mom again, too. At least the box they put her in. I sucked in a breath of air, and let it out slowly as I turned to watch them load the plane, mostly luggage. The train-like trucks had cars each attached to the next by something that looked like it wouldn't hold. I almost wanted the one train, moving kind of fast, to let go and throw suitcases all over the runway.

A stewardess came by and gave me these plastic clip-on wings, like the ones she wore on her uniform. Her name tag said *Judy*. Another stewardess came and brought me a brand-new pack of playing cards. My Nana had once taught me to play solitaire, but there never seemed to be a full deck to play with so it was nice to have a better shot at winning with those stiff slick cards with a funny plastic-paper smell. At least it gave me something to look at, something to concentrate on.

They offered me a pillow, blanket, and choice of magazines. I'm not sure if they knew I had just lost my mother. I got the feeling that they were always this nice, to everyone. There was something tiring about how cheerful and sweet they were, like the cheerleaders at my big sister's high school. Would these ladies be so bouncy if it wasn't pretty much their job? Who knew what they said later, when their feet were up at home, about that boy monster who just wouldn't stop screaming no matter what they offered him.

A woman sat in the aisle seat leaving an empty seat between us. I didn't say anything to her and she didn't say anything to me. I glanced out the window a few more times, as I tried to remember the rules to solitaire and moved cards around more just to touch them and feel their smooth surface than to put them in any particular place.

More and more luggage got loaded underneath. Just luggage so far. Part of me, maybe my own mother's voice still inside my head, said, "Don't look out that window. Don't watch them load the plane. Look away." Because I knew my mother was on that flight too.

Eventually Judy closed and locked the doors. She gave instructions for what to do in the event of a water landing. I was asked to put the tray table up. Everything had a slightly different name or was slightly smaller than normal. The bathroom was a *lavatory*, which sounded to me like *laboratory* and I wondered if anyone would be doing experiments in there. I did my own experiments with the tiny metal lid that covered the built-in ashtray of my arm rest, flipping it up, and back down, listening to the metal sliding click it made. I wasn't sure where to put the plastic from my new set of cards so I shoved it in there, enjoying the crinkly sound as I pushed it all in.

When the plane finally gave a jolt and started moving backwards, I looked out the window again, at all the little luggage trucks zooming this way and that. I felt kinda relieved that I didn't see my mother's coffin loaded, but I knew she was down there somewhere. I closed my eyes hard, hoping that would keep in the tears. Maybe if I held my breath. I pushed my forehead against the cold glass of the window, and let the tears go, blurring everything into soft shapes that weren't so scary.

I didn't want anyone to see me cry. That would've been embarrassing, even though I didn't know anyone there.

After what seemed like forever, the plane picked up speed and pointed its nose up in the air, leaving the ground as the rumbling of wheels on the runway disappeared into an eerie quiet hum. I closed my eyes and tried to block out that feeling of the bottom dropping out. "It's just like a roller coaster ride," I could almost hear Nana's voice trying to reassure me. "It'll be fun."

I tried to think of what my mother might've said to me and I couldn't think of anything. She would've put on a tough face, looked forward, and maybe said, "Be a brave girl." That's exactly what I did, as I imagined what the trip to heaven might feel like. I hoped it wouldn't include a bratty boy screaming his head off, and that heaven would look nothing like Newfoundland.

A few hours later, at my mom's dad's house, I whispered into the phone in the freezing hallway. "Daddy?" I hadn't called Bert that in years, back when he was still married to my mom. If only they'd stayed married. Maybe none of this would ever have happened. Then again, as my Nana used to say, "No point in frettin' over spilled milk."

"Mary? Is everything alright? Are you okay?"

"No, Dad, I don't like it here and I want to come live with you." I held the phone tight in my hand and too hard up against my ear, it made Dad's voice farther away and tinny. He couldn't be further away than he was at that moment, thousands of miles. "I want to come home."

"That's fine," he said, "I'll hop in my car and come get you. Are you still over there on Duncan, in that green and white house?"

He didn't know they'd shipped me off to Canada. Or maybe he forgot. Anyway, it was so nice to hear his voice. Memories of nicer times flooded back. My mother when she was still alive, when she was happy, at the kitchen table, the kitchen warm with the scent of hot apple cider, her and Dad helping me fix my Halloween costume, laughing and joking. Fun times. I didn't mean to whimper into the phone. I cleared my throat. "No, Dad I'm in—"

"Mary, what are you doing on the phone?" My grandfather—that I'd hardly seen before that day—came into the hall where I stood hunched over by the telephone stand. "No one said you could get on the phone. In this house, the rules are, you have to get permission first. Hang it up now. Kid, come on. You're not going to be a wild rapscallion when you're living here."

Rapsca-what? Who talked like that? No one I hung out with. And what's with all the rules? I ignored him and talked faster. "Daddy, I'm in Canada. I don't want to be here, I want to be in Buffalo with you."

Grandpa put his hand on the phone and gently tried to pry it from my white-knuckle grip. "I don't like it here, Daddy, please come get me."

"How did you get to Canada? Who are you staying with?"

We had a tug-a-war with the receiver. Grandpa's strength was too much, he won easily. Put the phone to his ear. I fought him but not all-out, not crazy socking or scratching, just shoving and grabbing. He put his big warm hand on my shoulder while he spoke into the phone.

"Hello, Bert. No, no, everything's fine here. She's only been here for a few hours and everything's new to her. Once she settles down she'll be fine."

I wanted to bite his leg. But that wasn't nice. I was supposed to love him. He was my mom's dad.

Grandpa listened for a moment then said, "No, that's not possible. She's not your kin, not by blood only by marriage. She belongs here with her ... family."

I figured he was about to say REAL family but he stopped himself. At least he gave some thought to how Bert would feel.

I could hear his voice all the way from Buffalo, crackling through that phone, getting louder. Nice to be wanted. Enough to cause swearing from another country.

"No, Bert, you have no right to talk to me like that. There's no reason for harsh words. The answer is no and it will always be no. I'm hanging up now. Good-bye."

The clank of the hard plastic phone in the cradle echoed in my head. I felt cut off from the only people who truly loved me. I slid down the wall, sat on the hard floor, cold on my butt because it was always too cold in Canada. Just a few hours earlier, when I got off the plane, the sky was gray with ugly shapeless clouds. Uglier than the gray sky in Buffalo somehow. Looked colder. My new world had strange buildings and cars and people without meaning.

Now it was dark and everything felt closed in on me. I cried. Grandpa didn't know how to handle it. He stood for a long time, his long leg next to me. I leaned over, took hold of it, held on tight. My tears dampened his pant leg. Had I run out of tears? He patted my head.

After a time he said, "You know what always cheers me up when I'm blue? I play the accordion. Do you want me to teach you to play the accordion?"

I didn't know what an accordion was. Sounded kinda interesting. But I wouldn't give in, I wouldn't say yes and go along with this idea of his, this baby's pacifier. Because that's what he was trying to do, pacify me, change the subject, to get me thinking of something other than going home. I wasn't a baby anymore and didn't want to be treated like one.

He gently took me by my arms and helped me up, his strength made me feel light as a feather. He was stronger than he looked. He led me into the living room and sat me on the dusty-smelling sofa, the back covered with white doily things. He went over to the piano, which for some reason had a roll of paper—with holes in it—attached over the keys. I wondered about that too but didn't ask.

He picked up a battered suitcase and carried it over. He sat next to me, the large suitcase resting on his knobby knees. I had to admit he was doing a good job pacifying, I wanted to see inside the suitcase, see what this accordion thing looked like. I was still mad at him for hanging up on Dad, for keeping me here against my will, but I had to see it. He knew he had my attention and after he flipped the two latches. He hesitated before opening it.

I held my breath until he did. A musty moist smell wafted up. I wondered how long it had been since that case was opened. Inside sat a miniature piano with "bellows" as he called it, in between black buttons on the opposite side. It was beautiful and odd at the same time. Like something from history or another world. Maybe somewhere in Europe, like in the movies.

He picked it up, moved the empty suitcase from his knees, set it on the floor and put the red velvet strap of the accordion over his head. He unhooked something and the bellows opened with a tired wheeze. He positioned his fingers on the piano keys, pulled the piano part, the bellows giving way, and played what he called a beer barrel polka. Maybe I'd once heard something similar on TV. He sounded like a real TV musician only better because he was right there. The music entered my body, rolled up and down and tickled. I smiled.

Grandpa liked playing his accordion. He closed his eyes and forgot I was sitting there. He played on and on. I could have sat there for a long time listening—but he'd originally offered to let ME play it. I tapped his arm as it moved back and forth manipulating the musical instrument. He opened his eyes, a smile in them. He wasn't a mean man. He just wouldn't let me go live with Dad.

"You said I could play it."

He didn't say anything, just leaned forward, took the strap over his head and put it over mine. "You hold it just like this, and push and pull, but you have to do it in long movements like this. Then you play the keys. I'll teach you the other buttons on this side after you get the hang of it."

I tried it. With the accordion right up against my body I felt the music even more. I played it for a long time, until the sun went down and the living room got dark. At some point Grandpa got up and left. I closed my eyes like he did when he played.

The light went on in the living room, I felt it behind my eyelids and I still played on. I learned the keys, the sounds each one made. Eventually, the novelty wore off and I again thought about going home. I wanted to go home. I stopped, opened my eyes, but no one was there. They had left me alone. They knew where I was because of the sounds from the accordion, knew I wasn't running away. That's why they let me play right through supper time.

I stopped when I realized they were working me. They were listening. I started up again this time playing bits of something I remembered. I picked out a few notes, missing at first, then found the right one. A simple song I learned long ago. One that got stuck in your head and wouldn't leave. One I wanted to stick in everyone's head in this whole stuffy freezing house. I got the notes, sounding it out, then I played and sang, "Gee Mom, I wanna go, gee Mom they won't let me go. Gee Mom, I wanna go, right back to Buffalo..." Over and over again, until they could no longer ignore me.

Chapter Three

Getting Back to Buffalo

My Canadian grandparents enrolled me in the local school, which at least I could walk to and I didn't have to take all those buses like in Buffalo. I didn't want to be there, and I didn't want to talk to anyone, and I definitely didn't want to do the homework. I complained about it but my mom's dad said, "No dinner until you finish your homework," and I was hungry so I did the stupid homework.

At least they did let me call my older sister. "Vivian, you gotta get me outta here. I don't know anyone and it's cold and gray—"

"It's cold and gray down here, too, you know."

My sister wasn't wrong. I changed the subject. "Why can't I stay with you? You'll barely know I'm there."

"You know I work two jobs. I don't have time to look after you and—"

"I don't need looking after. When did Mom ever look after us?" As soon as the words were out of my mouth, I felt bad. She had looked after us in her own way. Sometimes. Sorta. "I mean—"

"Let's not talk about Mom, okay?"

The second afternoon after school when I called her, begging again, crying a little, she at least agreed to talk to our grandpa.

After my third day of school, I headed for the hallway to call her again and my grandfather stopped me. "How much homework did they give you?"

"A little math and some reading."

"So why don't you knock that out right away so you'll be done? Your grandmother is making a nice roast for dinner."

I opened my mouth to protest, but I didn't feel like arguing either. Didn't feel like doing anything. At least the homework wasn't very much, and it wouldn't take me long, and I didn't really care if I did it right or not. Besides, I was already hungry and didn't want to delay dinner. The roast smelled good. Better than anything I'd eaten for dinner in a long time.

At the dining room table, I easily finished the math—they probably put me in a class below where I should have been—and read the short chapter. I slammed the book closed, louder than necessary. "Done."

The dinner smelled delicious and I quickly set the table. One of many chores Grandpa laid out for me to do, written in his nearly impossible-to-read handwriting on lined paper attached to the refrigerator with a "Gone Fishin'" magnet.

As I chewed the first delicious bite of the roast, Grandpa took a deep breath and smoothed the napkin in his lap. "We have something to tell you, Mary."

I stopped chewing. A few guesses flew through my brain that made no sense. *Your mom's not really dead, it was all a horrible mistake/trick/bad dream.* Silly kid stuff. *We've added a second page of chores to your list, including making dinner.* I chewed faster. That probably wasn't it either. I swallowed, remembering the scolding from the previous night to not talk with food in my mouth. "What is it?"

Grandpa sliced a piece of roast, and I wondered if he was stalling. "Your sister, Vivian, is going to have you stay with her for a while. You'll fly back to Buffalo tomorrow." He looked up from his plate, at my face, waiting for my reaction.

The first thought that popped in my head: *Then why did I have to do my dumb homework?* But more than that, I was relieved. And grateful. I set down my knife and fork and gave him a brief awkward hug. He patted my head. "We know it's been hard for you and we thought having your sisters nearby might make the... transition a little less painful."

I thanked them both, didn't complain about the stupid homework, savored every last morsel of that roast, then got up to pack my stuff. I practically skipped away from the table, but stopped myself since I didn't want to hurt their feelings.

The flight back to Buffalo was a bumpy ride. I didn't care. I was finally headed in the right direction. Home. Sisters and Bert, my best Dad, and my Nana. Life with my sister was a bumpy ride, too. We'd end up screaming at each other after just a few days. I'd stay with Nana a while, Bert for a bit, and the Martinez family—where Mama Lola was my other bonus mom. Lola always fed me and taught me how to knit when I was little.

The last part of junior high was a mess. I'd cut class and hit hockey pucks against a wall to blow off steam. Savor the alone time. Listen to the echo of the puck hitting the wall, making a mark.

My freshman year of high school was a bumpy ride, too, but I started to catch up, make a few friends, make peace with doing homework and with myself. It was the seventies, after all, and at 14 years old, I was nearly a grown-up.

Chapter Four

Dancing Queen

In 1975 in Buffalo, New York, you'd hitch a ride home as casually as you'd pull on a pair of bell-bottom pants. I liked to fly solo, do my own thing, and go to discos until after midnight with my fake ID that said I was 19 instead of my real age of 14. I felt like a grown up, making my own choices, doing what I wanted. Vivian was so busy with her own life that she wasn't paying much attention to mine, and that was fine with me.

I often thumbed a ride home late at night, by myself. I was young and fearless and the scariest thing possible—losing Mommy—had already happened.

My tomboy tendencies steered me away from those flowing brightly-colored dresses the contestants on *Dance Fever* wore, ones that swished gracefully when twirled. One night, I wore tight-fitting white bell-bottoms and a turquoise top with long flowing sleeves. Not too girlie but showing a few curves.

I preferred darker dance partners, maybe because Stan the Jerk used to say all kinds of bad things about black people, using the n-word all the time. I especially liked to dance with Marvin—one of the regulars, a few years older than me. His long, lanky, limbs moved so smoothly. His lighter-colored palms and long index fingers reached toward the ceiling. His eyes caught the multi-colored squares of light sprinkled over the dance floor by the overhead spinning mirrored disco ball. He could've plucked the ball from the ceiling and palmed it, as tall as he was at 6'8".

Marvin had finished high school and left for New York City, but came back to visit with tales of life in the Big Apple. He had this way of talking to me, low and in his deep, grown-up sounding voice. He'd look me right in the eyes, like he could somehow see all the way to my soul, see my loneliness and fears. He said, "Why don't you ditch this town with me. Come to the city." I'd thought about it. Buffalo held some bad memories with mom's death, and the city sounded exciting. But I had good memories here too, and my Nana, and Bert and my siblings. Plus Mama Lola and my calabash cousins in the Martinez family, full of love and always feeding everyone. They didn't mind if I showed up for dinner all the time. I'd also started working hard in school, even made the drill team. So I told Marvin no, but still danced with him and let him call me "baby."

He danced with other girls too, though. I didn't let myself feel too special. With people swirling and moving to Donna Summer and KC and the Sunshine Band all around me, I didn't feel alone.

On that one night, a couple other guys asked me to dance and I did, to the faster songs, Bee Gees, ABBA. "Dancing Queen" made me feel like I didn't need a partner at all—I was queen of everything, or at least my little section of the dance floor. "You can dance!" she promised us, even those dancing badly and singing off-key, "You can sing! Having the time of your life..." I worked up a sweat, my blouse clinging to me.

The music slowed down a notch, to Cher singing "Love Hurts." A guy in a yellow shirt with an especially large collar asked me to dance but I turned him down since I didn't want someone I didn't know getting that close to me, especially when I was somewhat sweaty. Not really my type, anyway. No one else there had moves like Marvin, who somehow made whatever he wore look like the next fashion trend, when on the next guy it might've just looked goofy.

In the ladies' room, I patted the sweat off my brow and re-applied some lipstick. I sat out a few more songs, watching the non-Marvin guys try the latest gyrations while balancing on platform shoes. Some had gold chains catching in exposed chest hair. Not smooth. Marvin played pool in the back, his arms almost as long as the pool cue.

I headed for the door.

I had rules about hitchhiking. If a car blasted music too loud and the passengers sounded too rowdy or drunk, I'd pull in my thumb and keep walking until a more mellow option came along. I was careful.

A green four-door boat of a car pulled up in front of me, no music and just one guy driving. I hurried to the passenger side. The bulky, heavy door took both hands to swing open. I glanced at the lanky black driver with nervous-looking eyes.

"Thanks," I said as I held my hands up to the vents on the dash, on either side of the glove box with cursive letters, *Impala*. He just nodded but said nothing. "Cold out th—"

A large hand covered my mouth from behind me, a cool blade on my neck. "Keep quiet and you won't get hurt," the voice demanded. The two I'd missed in the back seat barked the orders. My hands dropped. No longer cold, no longer feeling the warm air. Limp in my lap as time slowed and sped up at the same time. My mind raced for a way to escape.

I'm too young to die.

Chapter Five

The Wrong Way Home

My eyes darted from the driver to the one behind him in the back seat. Outside street lights faded into the ink-black night. My muscles tensed, pulling inward, holding tight, electrified but frozen. We drove further from the busy disco.

"Turn here," demanded the one behind me, with the knife.

The one behind the driver reached over the back of the bench seat and grabbed at my blouse. "Nice tits."

I stayed as frozen as I could. *Don't flinch.* Knife still at my throat. My mind spun. *Must get to other people.*

The hand on my mouth smelled ashy. He moved it, slow, seeing if I'd scream. He repeated, "Stay quiet and you won't get hurt."

"There's a motel back that way," I suggested. I pointed with my thumb. Could they hear the fear in my voice? Could they see through my ploy to get near people?

The driver glanced at ash-man in the rear-view mirror. "Drive!" he yelled, ignoring me. Grabby-man moved his roaming hands from my left breast to my left thigh. I pretended it was no longer attached to me. Just a leg in white bell-bottoms.

I looked into his eager eyes. "A motel might be more comfortable." And crowded with other people who could help me.

He wouldn't meet my gaze, just looked down my blouse. Hunger and greed flashed. No conscience. Pure lust.

"Pull in here," demanded ash-man.

A dead-end alley. *Dead. End.*

He killed the engine. Dim light from the street barely lit the narrow space. The back seat emptied. Ash-man whipped open that heavy door like it weighed nothing. The air smelled like a nasty dumpster. I scrambled toward the driver side, after the driver. Ash-man grabbed me by the front of my blouse and waistband. Pulled me from the car, onto the ground. I kicked. He pushed the knife to my throat, a warning.

"A feisty one!" cheered Grabby-man. He held down my arms. How many "ones" were there? Ash-man pushed the knife. The sharp edge stung. Blood slid warm, toward my collar bone.

I'm going to die.

I looked up to the sky, expecting a bright light. Tried to remember the words to a prayer. "Our father, who art in—"

"Stay still. Be quiet and I won't hurt you." He stared into me, seeing my fear, and dropped the knife to yank down my pants.

A bright flash of pain as he pushed into me. He rutted around like a beast. I looked away, tried to *be* away. A bright star in the night. I turned toward a white-wall tire next to me in the gravel. Dumpster wheel on the other side. My own pale-looking arm. Like it didn't belong to me. Grabby-man's strong grip. His throaty laugh. The driver leaned on the hood. I looked up into the night again.

One last violent shove.

"Yeah!" Grabby-man yelled like a crazed football fan. He pulled up his pants. Ash-man unzipped, kneeled on my palms.

Later I'd pick gravel out of the backs of my hands. Later I would find a dark cold void in my mind when I tried to remember their faces.

The driver came over next but couldn't do it. Didn't even unzip. He looked younger, not as mean as the other two. If it had just been him in the car, like I'd thought when I got in, I would've been home safe. In one piece. Not split up the middle. They dropped me off closer to my neighborhood. But I couldn't go home to my sister's house. She'd think it was my fault. Told me not to stay out so late by myself.

I found Hilda's house instead. Only been there a couple of times, a semi-friend from school. They came to the door, well after midnight, in robes with sleep in their eyes. Father, mother, classmate. I didn't have much to say much. They could see my torn blouse, held up to my shivering rib cage. The trail of blood down my neck. White pants ripped and soiled. They called Nana who came right away. She didn't blame, didn't make me feel ashamed.

At the hospital, one woman spoke in soft tones that floated through my dark haze. She dabbed at my neck, hands, knees with something that stung. I almost wasn't sure I could still feel anything. The bite of the sting brought me back to *here*. Now. Her eyes looked sad, and sorry for me. I wanted her kindness, but didn't want anyone to feel sorry for me, ever. I thought of my mother, who seemed to care about me only in moments like this. When I was hurting. Was Mom in heaven? Did she know what had happened to me?

The nurse apologized for having to examine my private areas. And the slow process of checking every bruise and scrape and writing it all down. Next, another lady in a different uniform asked me lots of questions. I don't think I gave very good answers.

Later, I'd learn what to remember. And what to forget.

She took notes when I told her all I could recall about the car, what they wore, what they looked like.

"The one with the knife—his hands smelled like ash," I said.

She nodded, but didn't write anything down. She looked at me hard, with her dark brown eyes that must've seen a lot of bad things. "This isn't your fault, you know." She patted my bandaged hand, gently. "Do you understand that? No matter what you did or what you may think, *this is not your fault.*" I nodded at the time, taking in everything through a fog.

But I didn't truly understand her words until much too late. I wouldn't believe those words for years. Maybe decades. Especially since Hilda, who I thought I could trust—her kind words and promises sounding sincere that night—would betray me and ruin my hometown for me, making it feel no longer like home.

Chapter Six

The next day at school

The day after that horrible night, I stayed home from school. Not that I had a home, exactly, at that point. I'd been crashing at Nana's or on the floor at the Martinez house with Mama Lola. My older sister Vivian was my official residence if the school ever called so I made sure that didn't happen. Most of the time. Vivian's sofa folded out into a bed with a mattress so thin you could feel the bars, so we usually didn't bother. I slept on the scratchy dusty-smelling bright orange plaid upholstery.

Vivian was extra nice to me but didn't know what to say. She brought me extra blankets. Soup. That kinda warmed my insides, but not the insides that hurt. Stung. Torn apart.

My head still felt fuzzy, everything around me in a fog, not quite the same reality as before. At least she didn't say, "I told you so" about the hitchhiking. I knew her holding her tongue and bringing me soup would only last so long. And the school would ask more questions if I missed more than a day. So I did my homework and got ready to face Hilda at school the next day.

Vivian gave me a ride so I didn't have to deal with the bus. Her car smelled like cigarette smoke mixed with over-chewed Doublemint gum. A little gross, and at the same time, familiar.

My shoes made the same noise as I walked down the main hall of Southside Junior High. Still, everything felt down a notch, like the volume on Vivian's stereo. Not so many glowy blue bars.

Then it went all the way up to full volume as soon as I saw the looks on their faces. First it was Sandra from the drill team, who normally had her nose in the air, acting like she was better than everyone else. When I went into first-period English and sat one row behind her, she did a double-take when I came in, and looked down, her eyes full of pity I was starting to hate. I pretended to look toward the window. She shot a look at Cindy in the next seat, who glanced in my direction, trying to act all casual like she was going to look my way anyway. My hazy turned to anger.

My neck got warm, my face broke out in a sweat. I thought my head might explode.

I knew two things for sure: Hilda had betrayed me, even though she swore she wouldn't tell a soul. My news was apparently just too horrible not to share. Also, if Sandra and Cindy knew, the news would travel to the whole school, if it hadn't already.

Vivian tried to cheer me up, telling me how everyone would forget as soon as the next bit of gossip went around school. "Besides," she added, "I thought you had all kinds of plans this weekend—didn't you say something about a fashion show at the mall?"

"Yeah, but I don't think I want to go."

"If you committed, you should do it," she warned, in parent mode.

"Whatever," I muttered, under my breath.

"Wasn't there a rumor that you might get to keep the clothes they give you to wear?"

"Who knows if that's even true," I replied.

"See? That's what most people say about rumors. You should go."

I still wasn't sure, but I did decide to hang out Friday night with my friends who were already out of high school, hoping they hadn't heard anything. That's where I saw Marvin, with his kind eyes, and his soft, deep voice, down from New York again, telling about how great it was. So this time when Marvin asked me again if I wanted to go back to New York City with him, I said, "Okay."

On Saturday, I decided to go to the mall for the show, not so much because I'd *committed* like Vivian pointed out, but since there was that small possibility that I'd get to keep the clothes, and what did I have to pack for New York? Not much.

Most of the girls in the show were from the drill team, which I was still amazed had picked me to be part of their group, in spite of my loner-tomboy tendencies. A few of them gave me pitiful looks or pointed while talking to each other. But then some rumor started circulating about how so-and-so might be pregnant. I hated to admit my sister might be right, but I wondered if there could be hope for me, after all.

The show was a blast and I loved being up on that stage, forgetting who I was for a moment and being someone else, more glamorous and confident. From the stage, I saw Marvin in the back, a head above the rest of the crowd, looking even more glamorous than any of us girls on the stage.

At the intermission, he came to the side of the stage and gave me a hug. "You looked amazing up there, girl, I'm so proud of you."

"I *felt* amazing, too." I smiled at him and noticed how a few of my classmates and a couple of my teachers were looking at me, like they were wondering about the tall handsome guy next to me. "In fact I was thinking, maybe I should stay here and at least finish the school year."

His sudden slap made my eyes water and face sting. I couldn't quite believe Marvin did it. Felt like slow motion. I looked around, stunned, unsure if that had really just happened. I caught the eye of the teacher in charge. Her mouth dropped open at the sight. For a second, I thought she might run to my side and haul me away to safety. Instead, she blinked a couple times, looked at Marvin with fear, closed her mouth, and turned to walk away.

I stared at Marvin in disbelief, my cheek throbbing. His angry look softened. "Oh I'm sorry baby, I didn't mean to hit you so hard. I just wanted you to snap out of that."

"I—"

"You know I love you, doll," he kept talking before I could get a word in. "I love you more than any of these people ever could." His voice was so seductive. But my face hurt. Was he a thug, too? "And I can protect you from all the... evil in the world."

We hadn't actually talked about what happened in the alley. Now I was pretty sure he knew. I also knew he had at least one other girlfriend. And how could he protect me all the time?

"You deserve so much more than all this," he said, gesturing to the now-little looking Buffalo mall, with the tinny piped-in music making it feel like something out of *The Twilight Zone*.

The teacher in charge called out, "Get your next outfits on, girls."

We'd already learned there would be no keeping the outfits. What other disappointments were in store for me here?

As if he could read my mind, he said, "In the city, you can earn enough money for all the outfits you'll ever want. Sheri will come get you in a few days." He turned and walked away. No doubt I'd do what he said.

In the backstage area I looked in the mirror and saw a dark red handprint on the side of my face. No one said a word. I was scared all over again. Scared of Marvin, did he really not mean to hit me that hard? Scared of this town and all the evil lurking in corners. Scared that the very teachers who were here to protect us and keep us safe, couldn't care less about me. The main teacher saw what happened and didn't do anything. How many others noticed the red mark and did nothing?

If I was going to get knocked down by the world, I may as well make money at it and get out of this lame town. Besides, most of the time I liked being around Marvin. He made me feel special. Maybe he just didn't know his own strength. I was scared to go against what he said, given how hard he could hit when he wasn't even trying. And excited to see the city.

I'd heard Marvin had been seeing a girl named Sheri for a few months, and she'd gone to New York City to work with him, but she was also from Buffalo. She was a few years older than me, around 17. He'd gone back to New York and sent her down for me.

I had long enough to say goodbye to the few people I would miss. I never wanted to talk to Hilda again. Or even see her face. At my sister's house, I packed some clothes in a backpack, and some shoes, makeup, and a shoebox full of pictures in a little purple suitcase Mom had bought for me at the Goodwill years before.

I couldn't face Nana. Not with the truth... which I didn't even know exactly. She'd want to know what I was moving TO in New York City. Mostly I just had to get away. Had to.

So I didn't give her a real answer about why I needed her to come by, just that I wanted the shoes I'd left at her house. She hugged me hard and looked into my eyes. "You know I will always love you." I nodded. She wouldn't want me to leave, would try to talk me out of my secret plans. I turned and looked away as she left. I'd miss her the most.

 I made room for that one last pair of shoes, and picked up this stuffed bear that my dad Bert, my only real dad, gave me back when I was four or five. Its paws were threadbare and one ear was missing. I held it against me. I'd told myself for years I didn't want to get rid of it because I didn't want to hurt Dad's feelings. Its musty scent calmed me and made me wish for those simpler, better days when Mom was still around and life hadn't gotten so complicated. Now I'd be living with a guy, a man, in a great big city. I didn't want him to think I was a child in any way. I left the bear in the hall closet of my sister's place.

Chapter Seven

How I Turned out

In normal *square* families, parents talk about how their kid *turned out* okay. I thank God every day my own daughter grew up into a beautiful, strong, intelligent woman in spite of the odds stacked against her from before she was born.

On the street, *turned out* means the first time a girl turns a trick. When people first hear about my background, they want to know about that moment especially, as though it's a line you cross. A switch you flip. Like someone is a normal person one day then a hooker the next. It's not that simple. Especially when that someone is a child who's already broken and desperate for love. Desperate for something that feels like home and a place to belong.

I know now that I was a prime target for Marvin, who started out in New York City as a shoe-shine boy where he learned about life on the street, and followed his older brother into the shadier parts of city life. I was a girl eager to please, and easy to please. Just a little attention went a long way with me. Even if he did have other girlfriends. He didn't hide this fact. All part of the process of getting me used to sharing him with others, and his sharing me with others. Looking back now, even the way he first got me to go to New York City covered his ass. He didn't transport me himself, instead he had Sheri take me, on a bus, from Buffalo to the Port Authority in The Big Apple.

This was in the spring of 1975. I was 14 years old. Just before Easter. I should've been looking forward to chocolate bunnies and dyeing eggs. Or Jesus. Instead, I looked forward to my own move to the heaven Marvin promised—the city that never sleeps, the shops, the famous people, the bright lights, and Broadway shows.

I would eventually see all those things and meet famous people. But the first ride from Buffalo to New York City was not too glamorous: a crowded Greyhound bus with Sheri, the other girl Marvin's friends also called his "girlfriend" or just his "girl."

We squeezed into a row near the front of the bus. She let me have the window seat. At the time I wanted to believe this was her being nice, so I could see the sights. More likely, she wanted to make sure I didn't get up and off the bus at one of the many stops along the way, have a change of heart or get scared. I didn't know any better to be scared. Besides, the worse things imaginable—my mom dying, a gang rape, and the betrayal of my friends—had already happened to me. I was relieved to leave all those memories behind.

I turned to look over my shoulder as we pulled out of the bus station, even though a little voice in my head said, "don't look back." I couldn't see anything away, the back of this bus had no window. Instead, the bathroom door that didn't quite close swung open and banged shut as the bus turned, fanning the stench of cleaning fluid and sewer.

Sheri didn't look me in the eyes. She watched all the other people on the bus. Even the driver. She wore heavy eye makeup that made her look older, and tougher. Her eyelashes at half-mast in a constant squint or like her mascara weighed them down. I thought her hot-pink tube top would be cold later, and wondered how she could sit in such a short skirt without flashing everyone. Her legs were so skinny she crossed them and tucked one foot under the other ankle. When she did look at me, she looked me up and down, a piece at a time. Her eyebrows pulled together at the sight of my shoes (comfortable flats), pants (my best dress slacks) and top (my favorite sweater set that was starting to pill but still super soft). She said nothing about my outfit, her expression both disgust and pity. I didn't care. I was headed out. Far away. Marvin said he'd buy me nice new things when I got there. He'd take care of me.

When the bus pulled onto the highway, and picked up speed, the trees flew by faster and faster. *I'm really doing this.* Vivian's face flashed in my mind. She shook her head when I told her I was leaving with little explanation. *You can't tell me shit!* I wanted to yell my sister who said I couldn't or shouldn't or ought not go. Needed to finish school. Was still a child. The bus sped up and felt like freedom. I could leave this place—all the shame, betrayal, horrible memories—and start a new life, if I wanted. "But what kind of life will it be?" I could hear Nana's voice in my head, even though I dodged that conversation. *You don't understand*, I wanted to yell. He *loves* me. He *gets* me. But I hadn't told them much at all about Marvin. Didn't know that much myself, really.

Who would I miss at Southside Junior High? No one. I could still visit my Nana. My sisters. I could always come home for a visit. Right?

"I'll be your mother, father, sister..." Marvin had cooed to me. Smoothing my hair. Calling me "Baby."

Tears welled. The bus felt too hot. I pulled off my cardigan, dabbed my eyes as I did. No one needed to see my tears. I pressed my sweaty forehead against the cool window. Shut my eyes tight. *No more tears.* I tucked the folded sweater against the window glass and imagined the bright lights of the city.

For that whole day-long trip from Buffalo to New York City, Sheri didn't say too much. Stuff like: "the bathrooms at this stop aren't that nasty, if you have to take a piss or whatever." She did drill one bit of information into my head, though. "You know some of what we do for Marvin's not legal, right?" "Sure." I didn't know exactly what we'd be doing for Marvin, but didn't want to look too stupid. Something about escorting people. Being a "pretend girlfriend."

"So if the cops stop you, don't tell them your real name, got it?"

"Okay." I liked the idea of having a new identity. Leaving my old life and old self behind.

"Use a common last name. Like Jones. Or maybe for you, Rodriguez. You look like you could be Puerto Rican or something."

"I speak some Spanish, too." I volunteered. At my home away from home, in the Martinez house, so much Spanglish flew around all the time that Nana would sometimes stop me when I used a Spanish word in her house.

"Zapatos?" she'd ask.

"Yeah, have you seen my shoes?"

On the bus, I stared down at my shoes. The thought of my Nana caused an ache in my chest. *Must focus on the future, not the past.*

Could I pick a new first name, too? I didn't ask.

"Forget your real birthday. Your new birthday is 5-2, '52. Easy to remember. Got it? Say it back to me."

"Five-two, fifty-two. Like the girl with 'eyes of blue.'"

"Like the *what*?" she squinted at me, not amused.

The lyrics, "Five-foot two, eyes of blue, could she, could she, could she coo..." swam in my head but I held it in. Along with everything else. "Never mind. Five-two, fifty-two."

Her cold stare made me squirm.

"May second," I added to show I had it. "Nineteen-fifty two."

"So... how old are you?"

I was already doing the math in my head when she asked. Eight years older than my real age.

"I'm twenty-two." I liked the sound of that. Not a teenager anymore. Not a *kid*.

"Good. Don't forget." She turned to face forward again. Done talking to me. Fine. I liked looking out the window at the trees and buildings flying by, not her annoyed face.

Later in the day, as the sky turned different colors, I thought of Nana's paint-by-numbers and what they might call each of the colors. Plum. Autumn orange. Passion pink. Never just the color.

The end of the day and of that old part of my life. Nana liked to say, "Today is the first day of the rest of your life." How long would her words echo in my head?

The closer we got to The City, the trees faded out and the yellow cabs popped up all over. More yellow cabs than normal cars. You hardly ever saw a cab in my Buffalo neighborhood, the suburbs. Unless someone was going to or from the airport. Like when my Italian maybe-Mafia ex-stepfather showed up when Mom died. Yellow cabs seemed scary and fancy at the same time.

I'd seen the city in lots of TV shows and movies but the buildings... they looked impossibly tall in real life. Much taller than any trees I'd ever seen. I understood now why they were called skyscrapers. I couldn't even see the sky for all the buildings and bright lights. Where had the stars gone?

As we pulled into the Port Authority bus terminal, Sheri pointed out the window to a big royal blue painted door on a building across the street. Large white letters popped out through the dark night: "Girls! Girls! Girls!" The hand-painted exclamation points looked festive. "That's our office." I didn't have time to process this information. The bus stopped and passengers gathered their belongings as Sheri hurried me off into the cool air.

Then there he was, Marvin, his warm smile. Those eyes looking right at me. Through me. He looked smaller compared to the big city, but still larger than life, larger than any of the normal humans standing near him. His long, strong arms engulfed me in a tight hug. "Welcome to New York City, Baby!" His eyes twinkled like stars, the only stars I needed to see. He loved me and that's all that mattered.

Chapter Eight

First Trick

Marvin's hug lasted about half a second. He stepped back, his expression serious. With a glance across the street and a nod, Marvin sent Sheri away. I was glad to have a moment alone with him, without his brother or "brothers from other mothers," who usually swarmed him.

He picked up my little suitcase. "Is this all you brought?"

"Should I have brought more?" I asked. Had I already screwed up?

"No, Babe, you're fine," he said, setting down the suitcase and holding my face in his big warm hands. "You're sooo fine, honey. You don't need nuthin' but me. I'll take care of you. Everything you ever want or need. Lots of fine things for my fine girl."

My knees felt weak. Not just from sitting all day.

"Okay?"

"Okay." I smiled my best smile. The song "New York, New York" played in my head. Mostly the line, "these little town blues... are melting away." Also something about "vagabond shoes," but I wasn't sure what that meant, exactly.

Marvin raised his long arm, his index finger up, just for a moment, and like magic, one of the yellow taxis zipped up to where we stood and a small foreign-looking man hopped out, opened the trunk and reached for my tiny-looking suitcase. I realized the taxi also looked small next to him—Marvin made everyone look small. The rest of us were like munchkins in the Wizard of Oz. As we piled into the funny-smelling, sticky-floored car, I thought of the line "There's no place like home" and how this glamourous city, and man, were MY home now.

"We're goin' to the Travelodge on 42nd and 10th, but take the long way, up Broadway," Marvin instructed the driver, then turned to me, brown eyes twinkling. "This gorgeous gal ain't never been to the city before. She should see the lights." I melted a little, along with my blues. This thoughtful detour would for sure cost extra. Riding in a cab was already an indulgence.

"Yes sir, to Broadway. Right away."

The cab lurched forward, zipped into traffic then stopped. Lurched forward a couple car lengths, stopped. Lurched again. Stopped. I didn't normally get car sick, tight circles like tea-cup rides and carnivals and spinning around until I got dizzy could keep me amused all afternoon. But this cab. I turned to look out the window and BAM! Hit my head as we whipped around the corner. "Ouch!" I touched the spot that hit. "Are we in a hurry?"

"Baby, this is New York," Marvin said, "everybody's in a hurry."

He touched my cheek again. Saw my distress.

"Hey man," he said to the cabby, catching his eye in the rear-view mirror. "No rush, we're just 'cruzin', you dig?" He pulled a folded bill out of who-knows-where, maybe his sleeve cuff? So smooth. I had so much to learn to live in this town. He made it look like magic tricks. A show. Flick of the wrist. Sleight of hand. He touched the cabby's shoulder and the bill disappeared even faster.

"Of course, sir. Here we are, Broadway!" He slowed to nearly a crawl. I stared out at all the people—so many people. Some in lines, waiting to buy tickets or maybe to be let into the show. So many shapes, sizes, colors of both the people and the outfits they wore. Like the whole world had come here for the big show—Asians, Europeans, Africans, South Americans, white people. They wore fur, sequin, animal prints... bell bottoms, halter tops, spaghetti straps, tuxedos, or nasty-looking overcoats on panhandlers. One lady even had an outfit on her dog, a little red coat to match her own, which matched her red shoes. I expected to see flying monkeys and munchkins any second.

At the Travelodge on 42nd street, Marvin got me a key to our room, and put my bags on one of those fold-out director's chair type stands next to the dresser.

"Did you want to change clothes or anything before we head out?" he asked. I didn't know where we would head out TO but didn't want to seem stupid or rat out Sheri for telling me nearly nothing during the whole bus ride.

"*Should* I change clothes? I don't really have that much..." I thought of all those flashy outfits I saw on Broadway.

"Don't worry, Babe, you're fine. I'll buy you whatever you need, whatever you want. Are you ready to start making some serious money?"

Tonight? I had no idea. It'd already been a long day and I could easily fall asleep right there on one of the two hotel beds with floral orange bed covers.

"Okay," I said instead. "Let me just freshen up a little." In the bathroom, I washed my face and reapplied the little bit of makeup I wore. Extra layer of lipstick. I stared at my own big brown eyes in the mirror. Squinted. Not wanting to look like a wide-eyed naive *girl*. "Be brave," I said to myself. "Strong. Grown-up." I made sure my slacks were zipped, and smoothed the wrinkles from sitting on the bus all day the best I could, and walked out to smile at Marvin. "Okay, ready." I hoped he believed me. I didn't believe myself.

As we strode down 42nd, just a couple of blocks back to where we'd caught the cab in front of the bus station, I had to hurry to keep up with him, about a stride and a half of mine to each of his. He stopped abruptly, like he'd been riding in those taxicabs too much, and asked: "What's your birthday?"

"Five-two, fifty-two."

"Good girl." He looked down the street and waved his hand like he was hailing a cab again but this time it was Sheri who came zipping up, still no smile, at least not for me.

"You show her the rest, Donnie's deal and all that, right?" he asked her.

"Yeah."

"Great, see you later." He touched me on the cheek, almost like he might pinch it, then walked away as fast he zipped there. I felt cold. Wished I'd brought more clothes. Wished he would've stayed with me for longer. Tears threatened to come but I pushed them down before Sheri could see.

Without a word to me, she turned and walked to the big royal blue painted door with "Girls! Girls! Girls!" in white. I followed her through the door and up some dark stairs, to a small landing with a tiny table that had a notepad and a little pencil, like the kind they use in mini-golf. A dwarf, with half his face smeared from a bad burn, sat behind the table. "Here's the sign-in sheet for the rooms. It's seven bucks for an hour. You give the money to him."

"You're Donnie?" I asked him.

Before he had a chance to answer, Sheri snapped, "Donnie's his wife, she owns the place. We don't have all day."

I tried not to stare at this man and his half-messed up face, like an Oz munchkin in a horror film. He didn't say a word, just held out his hand and stared at me, waiting. Sheri stared, too. I snapped into action and dug six ones and 4 quarters out of my purse. I had just one five dollar bill left. As I handed over the fee, Sheri gave me her final bit of training: "Keep your cash in your panties. Or coochie. Harder to steal from there. You might want a knife or something in that purse."

To the left were little rooms? stalls? corrals? sectioned off from each other with plywood. Each section had a flat piece about the size of a twin bed, also made of plywood, and covered with a grayish sheet that might've been white a very long time ago. I took all this in, still not completely sure of my "pretend girlfriend" role here. I struggled to shove down the fears I could no longer deny.

Sheri said, "Go pick a room, I'll snag you a customer but you find your own after this." She walked away. I glanced one last time at the dwarf. I dragged my tired feet and found a stall not visible from the door opening—thinking of a farm from a grade school field trip and how the conditions in those stalls were better. At least those animals had some fluffy hay to sleep on. I would have loved to curl up on a nice pile of hay, maybe next to one of those adorable baby goats, and sleep for a few days. Wake up back when I was a kid and my mom was still alive.

Sheri returned with an average-looking white guy. "He wants a blow job," she announced. She held out her hand and he gave her the cash. To me she said, "I'll just hold this for you while you take this one."

I looked at her, not wanting to look at him as he dropped his pants.

"You have what I gave you before?" She looked annoyed.

"Right," I dug through my purse again and tried not to look at the flesh banana that was there all of a sudden, unpeeled, and getting longer as he gave it a tug, looking kinda proud like he might say: "That's a nice one, huh?"

No one said anything. My stomach growled loudly, and I wished it was a real banana. No one had said anything about dinner, either. I put the condom on then looked at Sheri for further instructions. "Blow job," she repeated, like she was talking to an idiot. I'd heard the words before but didn't know what that was, so I guessed. I held his banana like it was the handle of a pinwheel, and blew on it like the tip might spin.

"What the fuck!" he yelled, pulling his hips back and the condom off. He glared at Sheri. "Is this some kind of a joke?" He pulled up his pants and walked out, still zipping himself up. "That *child* doesn't know... what the fuck!?" He gave me one last glance, his eyes full of pity. Sheri held up his money which he waved away, swearing all the way down the stairs.

Chapter Nine

BJ training

After my bad blow job, Sheri practically dragged me all the way back to the Travelodge, gave Marvin an earful, shoved me in with him, and slammed the door behind me. I held back tears again.

"It's not your fault, Baby, you didn't know."

He told me to ask ANY question, any at all. He said it so sweetly. Although I noticed he never apologized for sending me out so fast, with so little training.

I did have a question about some of the girls I'd seen on the street outside our office, as Sheri practically dragged me away, swearing under her breath. I noticed the ladies who wore the most makeup and were taller. They stood out from the crowd for real, and I figured they were not for-real girls. Men in drag. How did they have sex?

"Up the butt," Marvin answered. "Or they just jack off the other dude," he added. "In the dark, the guy can't tell anyway."

"So, some.... customers think they had, like, actual sex with a girl, but really got a hand just from another dude?"

"Yup, some dudes are dumb. Or they're so nervous and excited they cum right away anyway."

This gave me ideas. That whole rest of the night and as the sun was coming up the next morning, he answered my questions and had me try again and again, practicing the blow job thing on his thing. No condom. No hope of stopping my gag reflex.

"You never skip the condom on a customer you know, right?"

"Right." I thought, or at least hoped that having a condom on there might make it easier. Like somehow the slipperier thing would slide right past my gag reflex.

After what must have been at least a dozen tries, I still felt like I'd vomit. I sat back and held down the next-to-nothing in my stomach. I felt hot and cold at the same time, sweat on my brow. Marvin sat up and pulled me next to him, our backs against the headboard. "It's okay, Baby." He wiped my brow. "Take your time, you'll be okay." He rubbed my shoulder. "Take a breath."

I inhaled, wondering if I could flunk out of this class. Would he send me home? I couldn't go back there and face my classmates. Their pity. Their stares. Their betrayal. He looked at my face as though trying to read my thoughts. Seemed to really care about what was going on in my head. When was the last time that had happened with someone, anyone? Never with a handsome guy. "You know," he said, with a mischievous grin, "this is extra hard..." he looked down at his own not-so-hard anymore... thing. "I mean, extra DIFFICULT..."

I smiled a little.

"...because this right here is the biggest one you're ever gonna see."

I chuckled, and took hold again. It moved in my hand as if to say, "Hey!" Like it had a mind of its own. Like a little pet. Maybe that was the secret, to think of this male appendage like a separate, friendly, thing. Not like a banana, or a hot dog. Something not quite real like it was in a cartoon, with one big eye looking up at me.

"I ain't lying," he said when he saw me eyeing his thing in the eye. "This here is the finest, biggest—"

"Yeah, yeah, let me try again."

"Just see how far you can go, then try to go a little further."

"But is it true that most white guys don't have as big..." I started to ask. The botched customer from before wasn't this big, that was for sure.

"Not like I been lookin' at lots of dude's dicks, but the ladies always get all wide-eyed when they see this. And they say they never seen one so huge."

I wanted to ask, "Don't you think they might just *say* that?" Then I wondered how many women had seen it. I held on tighter, making a mental note of his size compared to my hand. He'd said earlier, "You're not going to break it," when I'd held it too gingerly. I thought again of that field trip to the farm where we each got a turn at milking a cow. Not that different, really. Yank and squeeze on this enough until the milk comes out.

When the sun was starting to come up and we finally fell asleep, I dreamt of that farm. My mom was still alive, a chaperone on the field trip. Cute baby goats everywhere. Chickens ran around, chased by little kids. A big red rooster clucked and cock-a-doodle-doo'd happily.

When I woke up, sun poking through the ugly hotel room curtains, I saw a *cock*, Marvin's, this time not looking at me. The eye pointed away and it didn't look so happy. Just deflated, and defeated, like I felt.

Chapter Ten

Italian Horseman

Those first few days in New York, I learned fast, and got better at talking sexy and milking men. Half the time I didn't even have to put it all the way in before the john came, or I used my hand like the dudes in drag. This body felt like it wasn't really... private or mine anymore, after the rapists in the alley. At least here I got money for it. Got better at pretending I was far away.

I made sure to tell each one what a big, beautiful penis he had. Almost slipped once and said *udder*. Because, in my mind, I was back on that sunny farm in Buffalo. Pretended I was back in school, and made a mental note of the size of each compared to my hand, like we had to when we dissected frogs. "Make a note of the size and color," said the lab book. "Did anything surprise you?" The variety of colors and smells surprised me.

The trouble started with an Italian customer who smelled vaguely of that farm I remembered from grade school. He folded his pants neatly then looked around for a place to put them. "Doe-vay?" he asked, sounding a little like *donde* the Spanish for *where*. When I didn't reply, he sighed and set them on the linoleum floor, so caked with grime and who-knew-what else you could hardly make out the original geometric pattern. He pulled off his boxers, folding them neatly and setting them on the pants. For a guy who smelled like farm animals I didn't expect the neatness. Maybe this was how he stalled, out of nervousness? Guilt? I wanted to believe at least some of these guys felt a little guilty about doing this. "Where do you work?" I asked, hoping to distract him enough to relax.

"*Con i cavalli*," he answered right away, then saw my blank look. "Horse-drawn carriage in Central Park. You know these?"

I nodded. "Oh yes, very nice." I'd only seen them in movies. Maybe one day soon Marvin would take me on a ride like that. Maybe for my birthday.

Back to the task at hand, I'd gotten faster each time with the condom. I'd also gotten better at finding something else to think about. Like how some of the kids at school called me "Mare," short for Mary. Seemed stupid since it wasn't much shorter, and I hoped I didn't look like a female horse. The song "The Old Gray Mare" popped in my head and wouldn't go away. "She ain't what she used to be," played a few times. Before I got to "many long years" my not-so-long customer was done with his ride. He reached for his pants but stopped. I sat up and looked to see what he saw. The neat clothing pile was not-so-neat anymore.

I'd heard some noises under the make-shift plywood beds during those first days, but figured it was just rats or mice. They were big rats—my coworkers! With greedy fingers in my customers' pants. Messing with the new girl. Now I was the one who got screwed since my customer would assume I *knew* the other girls were stealing under there.

I expected the Italian to start yelling. He said nothing, pulled his boxers and pants back on and took off down the steps.

He yelled a bunch of words as he got to the door to the outside. Sheri stuck her head out and we both peeked down the stairwell. "What'd he say?" she asked.

"Something in Italian?" For sure something angry.

He turned to look up the stairs and Sheri pulled us both back so he wouldn't see us looking. We heard the door to the street slam closed.

"We gotta go," she said, and dragged me down the stairs with her before I could ask why. She opened the door long enough to see the pouring rain outside. "Hold this a second," she said, handing me her knife. I stuck it in my purse with my own that Marvin gave me the day before. She pulled some cash from down below and put it in her own purse. She didn't ask for the knife back as she hurried outside and flagged down a cab in no time. A police car pulled up to the curb, too. Right next to the Italian customer. He gestured wildly at the cop. He turned to point to the big door with "Girls! Girls! Girls!" on it, then saw us.

"There!" he shouted. The cab Sheri hailed sped off without us.

"Fuck, fuck, fuck," Sheri looked around, panicky.

As the cop approached, I searched my brain for what I knew I was supposed to say. Name, rank, serial number? No. Fake name, fake birthday. I was no longer Mary Frances.

Chapter Eleven

Worst Summer Vacation Ever

In the back of that cop car, with my wrists behind me in handcuffs, I couldn't trust Sheri. She'd caused all this, and I figured she'd somehow blame me for the mess. "Marvin will get us out. Don't worry," she said without looking me in the eyes.

She sounded scared for the first time. Like she was trying to convince herself more than me. She didn't give a crap about my feelings. I took a deep breath, getting a good dose of the cop-car aroma, worse than most cabs: a blend of vomit and pee and misery. The floor, even more sticky than a cab. At least I could sit for a little while. My feet were killing me, and I hadn't seen any of the new clothes Marvin promised. I stared down at my feet. My baby toe stuck out the side of my right shoe. If I did have to go to prison, maybe they would give me different shoes to wear for a while. That would be nice.

I pulled into myself, trying not to feel the uncomfortable heavy shackles on my wrists. Not the type of new accessories I'd imagined for my future in New York. On TV and in the movies, handcuffs didn't look so heavy and sharp. "Keep your eyes down," Sheri ordered as we moved from one noisy place to another, to get our fingerprints taken, pictures taken. The cop had taken both of our knives. I figured we'd never see those again. Who knew what extra trouble they would bring me. Sheri probably knew.

When I did steal a glance here and there, the wide variety of people and outfits I saw were not as glamorous as those I'd seen on Broadway. Lots of yelling. Soiled, torn clothes. Smelled not much better than the cop car. Like in the movies, we got one phone call. "I'll call Marvin," Sheri said.

The uniformed officer who offered the call looked at me. "Anyone you want to call?" He didn't sound very concerned. He looked up when I didn't answer right away. I thought of my sister, of Nana. Glad my mother wasn't alive to see this moment in my life. "Well?"

"No. No one."

"Sign here."

I almost signed Mary. Wiped away tears. Hard to start the "Mar" without my hand automatically finishing it with "y." I thought of cursive class. Each letter carefully drawn out. Looked like a grade school kid's signature. I wished I was back there. A do-over. A place with fingerpainting and friends and recess. Nap time in comfy sleeping bags. A guinea pig in a cage.

The cage they stuck us in had no fluffy wood shavings. No water if we got thirsty. No friendly faces smiling at us. Just angry cellmates and a cold concrete wall and floor. I didn't dare try to sit on one of the benches, like Sheri did. She fell asleep like the whole thing bored her. I was too scared to look at the eyes of the other women and teens, but once I caught Sheri with her eyes just the slightest bit open. Was she faking sleep to avoid talking? Or did she actually sleep with her eyes open?

Eventually, I sat on the bench next to her, when there was room. The pain in my feet outweighed my fear of getting too near anyone. No one talked or yelled for a while and I listened to Sheri breathe, wondering what thoughts ran through her head.

The sound of metal clanging woke me. I sat up straight. Surprised I'd fallen asleep. My gasp of air, with the smell of urine and body odor, reminded me of my new reality. I had to poop, but no way was I going to do it in front of all these people on the can in the corner. At home, that was such a private thing you do by yourself, always with the door closed. I kept clenching, holding it in. Wondering if I might explode if I did it too long.

One of the women—or maybe she was just a girl, too, also faking her name and age—stood up. An officer confirmed her name. "You've been bailed out," he said.

She turned around as though checking her back one last time. Her eyes linger a second on something to my right and she cringed a moment. With all her makeup, I couldn't tell her age. But I could see relief in her tired eyes.

I glanced to my right to see what had made her cringe. One drugged-out woman was staring at her arm, picking at something. Was it a maggot that she pulled out and flicked away? My stomach clenched even more. Next to the maggot druggy, someone else was vomiting, maybe at the sight. A couple people groaned at the strong stench of rotting flesh mixed with bile. I looked away to the other corner of the too-crowded holding cell, and saw one girl with a lighter, flicking up a tiny flame to light her neighbor's hair on fire. "Fuck!" the other girl yelled and slapped at her own hair. The smell of the burnt strands mingled with the vomit.

As the bailed-out girl walked away, finally free, I wanted to ask Sheri if that would be us, soon. She sat up from her sleeping position and stared holes in the back of our now-free cellmate. I said nothing and looked down at my baby toe again. If only I had ruby slippers to get me out of here.

I lost track of time. The pain of my held-in poop overshadowed everything. After what felt like forever, but Marvin said was less than 48 hours later, he came with a lawyer in a wrinkled gray suit for our arraignment. The guy hardly looked at me or Sheri, just talked to Marvin, which I guess made sense since me and Sheri weren't the ones paying him. But I kind of hoped he'd at least ask a couple of questions. Like my real age. What had really happened. The Italian horse-and-buggy driver said we had stolen his money and raped him. I'd never heard of a male accusing a female of rape, but I didn't know what to think of any of this.

"You okay?" Marvin asked at one point, looking me over, gently touching my face. Making me melt a little with his big brown eyes.

I just nodded, afraid if I tried to speak I'd cry.

"Did she do okay?" he asked Sheri.

"She said the right stuff, if that's what you mean."

"Okay, good."

There wasn't much time for chatting. The court reminded me of when I went to Catholic church with Nana. An important-looking dude in the front wearing a robe. Lots of standing and sitting on too-hard wooden benches. A lot of words I didn't understand. No singing, though. I liked the part of church when everyone sang.

Bang! I jumped. The judge had used his little wooden hammer, like in the movies and the TV shows. "Forty days," he said. "Next case!"

I looked at Marvin, not sure of what just happened.

"Don't worry, Babe," he said, touching my cheek. "Forty days'll go by like that." He snapped his fingers, almost as loud as the judge's hammer.

"But—" Innocent people aren't supposed to— Was I innocent?

"Better than the seven years you could've gotten if you didn't plead," the lawyer said over his shoulder, in a hurry to get to his next case.

"Quit whining," Sheri said. "We all end up doing a little time. Not a big deal. Suck it up—"

Before she could say "buttercup" Marvin stepped between us. "They're going to take you now."

A couple of uniformed cops approached us. "I'll write you every day. You'll be fine."

"Maybe she'll learn something while we're inside," Sheri said with a sneer. "She's so fuckin' green."

The heavy handcuffs snapped on me again. Not quite as tight and cold and cutting this time. Just bulky and a little warm against my wrists and the small of my back. "This way, ma'am."

At first I didn't realize he was talking to me. No one had ever called me "ma'am." He guided me outside to a bus with "Rikers Island" on the sign over the front window. Dozens of handcuffed women lined up for this ride, all shapes and sizes. None smiling. All older and bigger than me. This was going to be the worst summer vacation of my life.

The bus reminded me of the old school buses I'd taken to various schools... before. An evil horror-movie or Twilight Zone version of a school bus, gray with black letters instead of the cheerful yellow. No signing. No talking allowed. I lost track of Sheri right away. She likely moved away from me on purpose. Fine with me. So far she'd done me more harm than good.

Once the bus was loaded, and moved away from the court and city, it jostled us hard, up and down over bumps and potholes on the disintegrating road leading to a long bridge in the distance. I leaned away from the barred window so my head wouldn't hit it on the bigger bumps, but not too close to my boney seatmate who looked half dead and stared straight ahead. I sat forward on the seat, my knees touching the back of the seat in front so the cuffs wouldn't gouge my back. I didn't want to touch anything.

The air smelled like body odor and diesel fumes. The view out the window matched my mood—gloomy and littered with broken buildings, rusted-out cars. No friendly faces.

Over the long, flat, boring bridge, we were off, not to grandma's or camp... this nightmare island greeted us with loud buzzing, alarms, and slamming gates. Yelling guards. Women screaming at the guards and each other.

We handed over our clothes, got searched and hosed down with something chemical smelling. Someone with gloves on did a "cavity search" to make sure we hadn't hidden anything in our butts or vaginas. At least she was quick. Less frightening than most of the customers I'd had so far. I feared the poop I held in so tightly would shoot out in her face. Kinda hoped it would. But her poking fingers somehow shoved the poop up there even more. I thought my insides would explode.

When she ordered me to get up, the energy and will rushed out of me. I had nothing left to hand over. No dignity, no pride or hope or strength. I dropped to my knees and hands. The stiff prison clothes scratched my skin. The awful floor, cold on the palms of my hands.

"Move it!" a foot slammed my left butt cheek. I pulled myself up, the n my pants, surprised I had the strength. Pain proved I could still feel . Anger. Hurt of all kinds.

When I finally couldn't take it anymore, and no longer cared about the lack of doors on the toilets, I had to use a finger to pull out the poop so hard and stuck in my butt. Something felt like it tore and my hand came away bloody. I still had to bare down to get those rock-like turds out of me. Thought I might pass out from the pain. Pushed out the last pebbles while I held in a scream. The hurt mixed with relief and cold sweat were odd combinations.

As the hours and days passed way too slowly, I wanted so badly to disappear. The kicks and smacks from guards and other inmates came often. I figured out how to hide or be invisible. Focus on the positive. The different clothes and shoes, not exactly soft or comfortable, at least got washed often and had no holes. I learned to appreciate very small things. Moments of quiet. A shower, even with no privacy. At least my body was clean and would not be shared with someone I didn't know. Food at regular intervals. Some of the food was better than others. I liked toast. I liked the people serving the food. Some of the people who worked chow hall actually acted as though they wanted to help us.

One day, one of the kicks I took from another inmate made me yell, "You broke my fucking ankle!" loud enough, over and over, until I started to go hoarse. The guards hauled me off to the infirmary, maybe just to shut me up. The nurse who examined me had kind eyes and reminded me of my Nana. She gently held my leg this way and that. The sound of my own yelling still echoed in my head. Didn't sound like me, or at least not little Mary Frances from Buffalo. Now I was Maria, for better or worse. Forever?

"Does this hurt?" her voice floated by me. "Maria?"

"It all hurts," I said softly.

"Well, it's not broken."

Panicked they'd send me back out there, I spat out more words. "Aren't you going to X-ray it?"

"No, it's just a sprain." Her brown eyes had pity in them. I didn't want her or anyone else to feel sorry for me. I stared at the colorful flowers on her scrubs, and looked around at the quiet room with comfortable beds.

"Can't I just stay here for a little while longer?" I wanted to add, *I'm just a kid, and my birthday's coming up*, but Maria's birthday had just passed, and little Mary Frances didn't exist anymore. That would get Marvin in a lot of trouble, and then what?

"Sure. I'll get some ice for you to keep the swelling down. You're too skinny. I'd hate for you to miss dinner, so how about you stay until then?"

"Ok. Thanks."

I pulled that *I'm sick/hurt* trick one too many times. The guards started ignoring me like the girl who cried wolf. I volunteered as a trustee to work in the kitchen, like KP duty in summer camp. I didn't mind cleaning, especially if it kept me back in the kitchen, away from the meaner girls. And this nasty floor, on my knees scrubbing, was far better than that nasty floor in the trick house that no one ever scrubbed. My skin crawled at the thought of bodily fluids from who knew how many johns.

I pretended to be Cinderella. I had yet to hear from Marvin or get any of those letters he promised to write every day. Except for one, but it didn't make too much sense, like he was high or I missed a previous letter. I wanted to believe he still cared about me. And would come to my rescue like Prince Charming with a glass slipper. I wanted to believe that fairy tales could still come true.

"Mealtime's over! Back to your cells."

Yelling always pulled me out of my daydreams.

On my actual birthday, my second week, I was in the kitchen doing KP, when a fight broke out in the food line.

"Bitch! Who do you think you are?"

Trays clattered to the floor, food and metal dishes everywhere. A huge female, yelling and swinging fists, stopped for a second, arms loose at her sides. My legs, on autopilot, moved me closer to the mess on the floor, mine to clean. She caught my gaze.

"You wanna piece of this?"

She shoved her way into my corner of the kitchen. I ducked by the metal sink. A guard grabbed her wrist mid-swing.

I held in tears. My *birth*day would be my *death* day. A cold fear froze me as the mountain of a woman fought and swore, pulled away by two guards. I eyed the hard metal sink edge, took a deep breath, and whacked my wrist, landing on it with all my weight. Loud crack. Pain radiated. My arm now bent at a weird angle. I'd done it. No way anyone could claim it wasn't really broken. Cold sweat covered my skin. I slid to the floor, cradling that arm. Spots filled my vision, and then there was nothing.

My nose tingled with the scent of Lysol and alcohol. Bright lights made me want to open my eyes but not too much. White walls with colored posters, not yet in focus... so much more pleasant than the dreary gray walls and stench of body odor and feces. I inhaled a deep breath. My arm hurt but felt somehow softer, here in the infirmary. Fur. Like I was in fur. And merry. Floating. Had they drugged me?

A nurse in plain green scrubs appeared. "Glad to see you're awake. You broke that arm pretty good."

"Thank you." I realized too late she didn't mean I'd done a good job breaking it, even though I had done a fine job. Quick thinking enough to break the left one, not my right. If I did say so myself.

"We gave you something for the pain and set it while you were out. But you still need a cast to replace that splint."

"I get a cast for my birthday." Almost forgot it was no longer my birthday. I was no longer Mary. "A whole cast of characters, maybe they'll act out a play here on this comfy bed." Let her think I was confused. I'd have so many more broken bones if I accidentally ratted out Marvin.

She squinted at me. "They're going to put a plaster cast around your wrist," she said real slow.

"That sounds good. Will you sign it for me?" Isn't that what happened when you got a cast? Everyone signed it like an autograph book on your arm or leg or whatever got hurt.

"Sure, hon, I'll sign it. Just has to dry a little first."

My broken arm didn't even keep me in the infirmary overnight. The nurse who promised to sign my cast left at the end of her shift. Fine. It would've been dorky to have her sign it anyway. The weight of it surprised me. I now had my own bat. Should've broken my right arm after all.

"What the fuck happened to you?" Sheri appeared out of nowhere at dinner that night. I flinched but didn't jump. Hoped she didn't notice.

"Broke my arm."

"I can see that, dumbass. How'd you do it?"

I looked away, scrambling for a better story than *I broke it myself to avoid all this*. Although that was pretty badass, to me anyway. "I fell."

"Right. You keep telling that story. At least now you have a place to keep a knife."

That hadn't occurred to me. Not sure if she meant in Rikers or after. "Have you heard from Marvin?"

"Yeah, all the time, haven't you?"

I shook my head.

"He sent *me* letters and money. Oh, you know what?" she slapped me on my shoulder. "There's this other inmate named Maria Rodriguez, almost forgot. I heard her say, 'Who the fuck is Marvin?' last week so I looked over her shoulder. She had a good laugh at the letter. Chuckled and said, 'Thanks for the cash, Marvin, I love you, too!' Funny, huh?"

I'd tried so hard to have thick skin. Let hard looks and rude comments bounce off. Didn't always work. My face turned red at the thought of the other Maria laughing at my letter and stealing my money. I turned and walked away from Sheri before tears or any fear showed up on my face. The drugs had worn off and my wrist throbbed. And itched. I held it close to me. At least Marvin had written to me after all, and sent money. Wrote that he loved me? Sheri might've made that up just to mess with my mind. Right? Would she?

I tried not to think too much about crap I couldn't do anything about. Pass each day with my head down as much as possible. I spent as much time in prison classes as I could, happy all over again that I broke my left arm and not right. My favorite class, art, was mostly drawing. They made sure all the pencils were accounted for at the end. One of the drawings I did was a landscape with lots of hills and trees. They liked it so much they used it for the cover of the newsletter. That made me feel slightly better, like there might be some hope for me.

Until other inmates trampled it. "Oh, the fancy artist, thinks she's special."

I didn't feel like drawing so much after that. Just squares over and over. Like the cells in the prison.

When I finally crossed off that last tick mark-slash—the whole, long 40 days—and they let me out, my own crappy clothes and shoes and no smell of Pinesol gave me such relief and so much joy at my new-found freedom, that I forgot much of what I had learned. Maybe my brain just blocked out all of it, wanting to forget the whole thing. Like it never happened. I was sprung and happy and free like a bird.

Chapter Twelve

Big Cop

On the bus away from Rikers Island, back to reality, I sat next to the least-scary-looking girl. She might've been just a girl, too. Small. Wide-eyed. Holding her possessions on her lap like she was coming home from summer camp, not prison. She smiled sweetly when I sat down next to her, said, "Hi."

"Hi." I didn't recall seeing her on the inside. Didn't remember her face. She might've figured out even better ways to hide.

"Where are you headed after this?" she asked.

"Just back to my, uh, boyfriend."

She gave me a look. "You mean 'pimp.'"

I sat up, startled. How did she know? How could she just say it out loud like that? A tear formed in the corner of my eye, luckily the one away from her. I hated myself for it. I knew better than to show fear or weakness. Of all I'd learned in prison—that was the biggest lesson. *Show no fear.* I wiped it away, hoping she didn't see.

"It's okay, we've all been there," she patted my leg softly. "I didn't mean to upset you."

"It's okay. You're right I—"

"You just don't know what to do," she interrupted. "You don't know how to get away, right? You're not sure he really loves you?"

Her words exhausted me. Forced me to think. Marvin *had* finally come to see me. He explained how he had been writing to me, and how that other Maria Rodriguez got my letters and money. How he loved me and was so proud of me and how I was brave and smart for breaking my own arm. His eyes twinkled like in those early days when we first met each other. When he promised to save me and take me away from the nightmare that Buffalo had become for me. He did take me away. He did love me in his own way. Right? Had my own mother ever told me she was *proud* of me?

"Doesn't matter," she continued, "we're in the Big Apple! This is America, the land of opportunity! If you can make it here... shoot if you can survive Rikers Island, girl, you can do anything!"

I liked the sound of all that. "I like going to shows."

"Forget *going* to shows, why not *be in* a show, you could be a star, you could be anything you want." She talked low, whispering like we were on a school bus as kids conspiring, telling secrets.

I didn't think about the fact that the word "conspiring" has the word con in it and how much words can screw with our brains. She knew just the right words to say to me, just what I wanted to hear.

Not until much, much later—decades—would I realize she was doing a miniature version of what the men who "loved me" did to get me to do exactly what they wanted.

I followed her to a hotel room, eager to hear more about how wonderful I was, and how great things were in my future. I foolishly left all my possessions including the most money I've ever had that was all mine—about $50 for the KP duty I did in prison—just there on the counter next to the sink. In the short time I sat there on the toilet, she snatched the cash and was long gone. I now had exactly two dimes on me, 20 cents to my name. I wanted to cry and laugh and bury my head in shame, all at the same time. Run to the police... for what? To tell them... take me back to prison, I made more money there.

But I knew that wasn't true. I had seen how it was possible to get hundreds of dollars off of one john, one trick. This girl, this con woman, had taught me the most important trick I could learn at that point in my life—not how to actually *screw* someone, but how to screw with their mind. I suddenly realized that was how I could survive on the street and make as much money, more money, than Marvin could ever spend. Or so I thought at the time.

I smiled and said exactly what my customers wanted to hear, just like the girl on the bus from Rikers Island had done to me. I talked fast and moved my hands even faster. I could pleasure them and sometimes pick their pockets like a magician. Even with my one arm still in a cast. I practiced picking pockets with my toes until I had it down cold. No way was I ever going back to prison and no way did I want to touch any part of them any longer than necessary.

I got faster and made more money than any of the other girls, and Marvin was thrilled. The girls were not, so I still kept away from them as much as possible. But one night three Chinese tourists wanted three of us girls, so I had to work with a couple of those so-called *wives-in-law*. We went to a nasty trick house smaller than the Girls!

Girls! Girls! location but not as divided up. We paired up and collected our money.

"Everybody, hands up!" yelled a druggy crazed creep in the doorway, waving a gun. The Chinese tourists followed the other girls and put their hands up. The druggy waved his gun and took the guys' wallets, yelling for us all to get naked. The guys looked so scared. I'd seen the druggy before. He must've followed us. I hated this but feared Marvin much more than this skinny loser. I slipped my cash in my snooch while taking off my clothes, and told him my guy hadn't paid me yet. The druggy spent extra time looking inside my cast from every angle, sure I'd stashed something in there. Idiot. Luckily the tourists had enough cash that the druggy creep didn't care so much about not finding any money on me.

I felt almost sorry for the guys, they looked so terrified, and Druggy still didn't leave. Damn sicko wanted to watch. Or have sex. He didn't even know what he wanted. The Chinese guys scurried off and he had his way with the other two girls.

"I'm pregnant," I claimed, "so how 'bout a blow job?" This worked most of the time. Druggy nodded eagerly and got mostly a hand job. I'd figured out how to keep my head in the way so the guy couldn't see exactly what was going on.

When he finally left, with the other girls' money from almost a whole shift, we went to Marvin with the bad news, expecting him to go after the guy. One of the girls knew where he hung out.

"How could you lose all that money!" he yelled, socking the other girls, full in the face and in the stomach. He turned to me.

"I didn't lose mine," I said to him, holding out the cash. He yanked it from my hand, and smacked me anyway. My face burned from the hit, the betrayal, and the unfairness of it all. I wanted to yell, *I didn't actually have sex either*, but the smacks kept coming, and I knew it didn't matter. It mattered to *me*, though.

"You two better get back out there, work a double shift and earn that money back," he yelled, kicking one in the butt cheek. They looked more defeated than pissed. I was so mad I thought my head might explode. Mad at Marvin for being unfair. Mad at the girls for not stashing their cash. Mad at the thief. Mad at the world.

Outside on the street, none of us were in a big hurry to get back to work. I was too pissed to see straight and had to do something.

I turned to the girls. "Where did you say that asshole druggy thief hangs out?"

The one girl pointed to the bar on the corner. "What are you gonna do? You can't do anything."

"Let's go scare him, at least," I demanded. Maybe we couldn't call the cops. Or get our money back, because he'd probably already spent it. But we could make him think twice about doing that ever again.

I touched the knife I kept tucked inside my white trench coat, and turned on my heel, headed to that corner bar. Behind me, they scurried to keep up. "What do you think she's going to do?" I overheard one ask the other.

"I dunno, she's nuts."

I shoved the bar door open, stepped inside and spotted him right away. When he noticed us, he wiped beer foam off his mouth and pretended to shoot guns with both his fingers. "Ha ha got you all," he bragged, slurring and laughing. "That wasn't even my gun and it wasn't even loaded."

In one smooth motion, I pulled the knife out of the coat and pressed it against his neck, surprising us both. "Look you little shit-ass, try that bullshit again and I'll slice your head off." I said it with such conviction that his eyes went wide and he held his hands up.

I let go and walked out as fast as I'd come in. The girls hurried to keep up behind me. My bravado melted away as fast as it had come on, and I worried he'd come after me, maybe this time with a real weapon... or a cop.

I half-ran and ducked into a subway entrance so he wouldn't see where I'd gone. It was well after midnight by this time so the subway was closed, just the stairway not closed off. The two girls followed behind me. I thought they might, maybe not exactly give me high-fives for what I did or thank me, but somehow acknowledge my badassness.

They whispered to each other as I caught my breath. The older one smiled, kind of a fake-looking smile, and asked, "What kind of knife is that? Were you really going to cut him?"

"Honestly? I don't know what I was going to do. Just wanted to scare him, really. This knife," they leaned back as I pulled it out, "no, it's not even very sharp."

"Get her!" the older one yelled. The other held me against the wall, my right hand to one side, my cast slammed the wall on the other. My cast cracked against the wall, maybe the wrist, too.

"Hey! What gives? I got no beef with you," I yelled.

The older one pulled out a real knife, sharp and shiny. My throat went dry. "But we got a beef with you," she said.

"Let me go." I struggled to get away.

"You're not going anywhere, ever again."

Betrayed again. I yanked my hands free. Squirmed, dropped to my knees. Tried to block the blade. "Nooo!!"

She drove the blade into my arm. Searing pain. I slid to the ground. Blood soaking my white trench coat. Her eyes flashed pure evil and hate.

"I don't wanna die!"

"That's what you get," she raised the knife again, almost dropping it, slick with blood, "for makin' us look bad." She drove it in again, higher on my arm. The pain extreme.

"Stop!" My vision blinked in and out.

The younger one said, "We gotta go. They'll send us away for a *really* long time for murder." They took off.

I wanted to yell *Bitches!* but could hardly breathe. Knew I had to get up on the street. *Must get help*. Crawled, blood everywhere. White coat turning red. Hot. Slippery. Made it to the top step. People all around. "Help me," not sure the words came out but people hurried away. *No one stopped*. I'd die right here all alone on a busy sidewalk. *Please, God, don't let me die like this*. My vision faded again.

"Oh my God, what happened to you?"

I looked up into the familiar face of "Mad Dog" the cop who hated all the girls but for some reason liked me. His hair stuck out from his head like a halo.

"Am I dead?" I tried to turn over.

"Holy shit you're bleeding real bad, hold this right here," he pushed my hand down on the wound. I flinched but held on, determined to live. He scooped me up and into the back of a cop car, yelling for someone to, "Drive, drive, drive!"

Chapter Thirteen

Little Cop

Marvin's face had never looked so worried. As I came to, and looked around the hospital room, I felt the pain in my chest with a weird pulling sensation. He held my hand. Weird. He never did that.

"Baby, I thought you were dead."

"Me, too." My voice cracked and my chest hurt more from the effort.

"What the fuck happened?" Behind him I saw those two bitches, both shaking their heads and holding their fingers to their mouths, like "shh" don't say a word. They looked terrified.

He squeezed my hand, "Never mind, tell me later, you just relax and get better. But I wanna know who did this to you."

When he got up and left the room, they begged me so hard not to tell him what they'd done. They'd been so sure I was dead, I knew I would never have to worry about them messing with me again. Too scared I couldn't be killed, or that Marvin would beat them near to death for trying. I should've been dead. Somehow God, and Mad Dog the cop, had my back.

One night soon after that, while I still had stitches in my arm and my cast from Rikers, another cop intervened in my life. A little Italian cop started asking me questions right there in front of Port Authority near my usual spot on 42nd Street. What was the deal with me and Italians? I guess I might've looked Italian, especially with my black hair, which wasn't so black anymore—the dye job from back in Buffalo had faded like my innocence.

This small cop stood with his feet apart and hands on his overloaded belt buckle, but even with this puffed-up stance he wasn't very big, barely taller than me, and a little less scary because of that.

"What are you doing out here so late at night?"

"Nothin'. Why, did I do something wrong?" I asked, violating the don't-talk-to-cops rule right off the bat. But I didn't understand why he was talking to *me*.

"How old are you, anyway?"

"Twenty-two." *Wait, was that still true? I'd had my birthday inside, but that was my real birthday...* I'd need to double-check my math later. At the moment I had to keep myself out of trouble.

"Uh-huh. What's your birthday?"

"Five-two, fifty-two." I hoped I had that math right.

"I see. Easy to remember." He didn't sound like he believed me. "How about you come with me across the street for a minute?"

"Why? Am I in trouble?" I asked, checking around for corners and nearby alleys where I might flee.

"No, you're not in trouble. I promise I'm not going to arrest you. I just want to make sure you are who you say you are... so you're safe." His brown eyes looked at me hard. Like he meant it. When I hesitated he added, "I'll get you a soda and a snack, too. When's the last time you ate something?"

I couldn't remember.

"That's what I thought. Come on, we'll just have a little break right there in that room across the street." He pointed at a bright window under the sign for the Port Authority Police. Did he think I was a runaway?

"Ok, but I only have a few minutes."

When I sat next to his desk, he smiled and opened a big drawer. "Chips? Twinkies? What sounds good?"

My eyes went wide at the stash. A whole drawer just for snacks.

"How about both? I'll trade you for a quick peek in your purse there."

I hadn't gotten a replacement knife. There was nothing illegal about having baby wipes and condoms, right? I eyed the stack of snacks he'd piled in front of me and handed over the purse. When was the last time I'd had a Twinkie? My teeth sunk into the fluffy cake and creamy heaven in the middle. My new Italian friend poked around in my purse. And pulled out the tiny address book I'd forgotten was in there. Should NOT have been in there. Marvin would be pissed. I stopped chewing.

"You're okay. Was it 'Maria' you said?"

I nodded.

"Did you want an orange soda or something to wash that down?"

I nodded again, wondering what he was going to do with that address book.

"Hey, Jones," my Italian cop buddy called out to a guy across the busy room, "grab us a Fanta, will you?"

Fanta sounded so fancy.

"So you won't mind if I call a couple of these people to make sure they all know where you are, right?"

If I could sit there and keep eating Twinkies, I didn't care. I chewed faster, swallowed the last of the first Twinkie, and opened a second while I still had the chance. "Some of those people call me by my English name, too, Mary. You know, the gringos."

"Sure thing."

A couple of the people he called, old teachers, old friends, just confirmed something like, "I heard she'd moved to New York City."

Then he called Vivian. My sister. I swallowed hard.

"Sorry to wake you, Ma'am. How are you related to Maria? Or Mary?" He paused while he listened to her answer, and looked at me. "I see, you're the big sister. So you could tell me her birthday."

I looked away, hoping I'd still get to keep the snacks. And he'd keep his promise not to arrest me.

"Just turned 15, is that right? And how did she break her arm?"

Now her voice was loud enough to be heard through the receiver, demanding she speak to me.

"Sure, I can put her on the phone, she's right here."

I waved it away. Didn't want to talk to her. Didn't want to have to explain.

"Uh, she doesn't want to talk to you for some reason."

More yelling. "Pleeeease convince her to come home to Buffalo!" He turned away from me so I couldn't hear as well. The yelling surprised me some and made me feel loved that she would care enough to raise her voice—to a cop.

"Hang on a sec." He covered the receiver and looked right at me. "She's really worried about you. At least say hello so she knows you're alive and I'm not holding you against your will or anything."

I held my hand out for the phone. "Hi Vivian. I'm fine, really."

"You broke your arm? Did Marvin do that to you? Are you okay? Why are you out so late and why did that cop stop you?"

"I'm fine, really. I just tripped on a curb. I was out ... seeing a show. You know how I love Broadway shows." What would she say about the stab wound if she knew about that?

"By yourself? Where's Marvin? He shouldn't let you—"

"I'm fine, really. Don't worry."

"I *am* worried, I..."

I handed the phone back to the Italian.

"She seems fine. But I wonder if—" he looked over at me, as if trying to read something in my facial expression. I started to open a third Twinkie, because you just never know when your snacks might be taken away. Jones came over, opened that Fanta and sat it on the desk next to me. The condensation glistened like in the ads. I took a long gulp. "I wonder if she might rather be with you than here."

I shook my head.

"You know, just until her arm heals. So you can look after her."

That didn't sound SO horrible. I remember how nice she was after my attack, letting me stay home from school. Checking my bruises and making me soup. That sounded a lot better than going back across the street.

"There's a bus leaving soon for Buffalo."

Somehow this little Italian guy talked me into getting on a bus for my sister's house. He arranged for the payment, a prepaid ticket that my sister was gonna wire money for. I don't know how he did it so quickly. By the time I came to my senses I was sitting there on the bus with only a bag full of snacks. I had zero cash since I'd just started my second shift after giving Marvin all my cash from the first shift. I didn't know what the hell I was thinking, listening to a cop.

I had learned the trick of stalling while boarding busses, hanging back about half way through the crowd, so that I could choose which person I sat next to instead of being the first on board, where who knows who or what might sit next to you. Again I chose the skinniest, tiniest person—the one least likely to do me harm—as my seatmate.

As the bus pulled away from the Port Authority, I knew I couldn't go back and face my sister. What would I tell her? How would I explain everything I'd done since moving to the city? Besides, Marvin knew where I was from and would find me and beat me senseless if I actually did this. No way would he just let me *go home*. There was no home to go to anyway, after what Hilda did to me. Everyone already thought I was ruined.

If I wasn't gone too long from my shift, I could easily explain to Marvin how that cop got ahold of me and forced me to get on a bus. Better yet, I could walk back to my usual spot and still make enough money to keep Marvin from being too pissed at me or even noticing I was gone.

I hoped the next stop would be in just a couple of minutes like the city buses so that I could still walk back. But this was no city bus, this was a Greyhound. The minutes kept passing with no stopping. I thought about whether or not it was possible for me to jump from a moving bus. I was pretty sure the bus driver would have to open the door for me and would stop me from doing anything. Because the nice Italian cop had given him the lowdown on how I was what, a runaway? I didn't hear the conversation. I was already seated halfway to the back when I saw them talking before we left.

More miles passed with no stops. I wasn't even sure where I was anymore, and the low lights inside the bus made it hard to see out. Each time I looked toward the window I saw a stranger in the reflection. Some girl who looked tired. Didn't even recognize her at first until I spotted the cast and realized it was me. I looked tougher. Like I could handle this adult life without having to run back to school and big sis to look after me. I could look after myself. Well, with Marvin looking after me.

Finally, the bus stopped and I waited until the driver was off, collecting tickets of the new passengers boarding. The streets didn't look familiar at all but at least it was still in the city and I spotted a yellow cab in the dark. I crossed the street so the bus was between me and the bus driver. The cabby gave me a look when I said I needed to go to 42nd street.

"That's a long way from here." The older, wrinkly white guy reminded me of some of my grandpa's friends.

"I know. If you could hurry that would be great. I'm late." Tried to sound confident. Didn't want him to suspect I had no money.

He pulled away from the curb, not so fast, and kept asking me questions.

"How old are you, anyway?"

How many times would I get this question in one night? "Twenty-two. I just look young. Especially with this cast."

"I see. How did you break your arm, anyway?"

I needed a better, more real-sounding story than "I tripped" which was code for "I'm not a rat." Something more grown-up, and like I had money. I cleared my throat. "Horseback riding. The horse didn't like me."

"I see." He said again.

I hoped this cabby wouldn't throw me to the curb and break my other arm because he didn't like me either. We made more small talk for a while until he grew tired of saying "I see" which I suspected was his code for "Bullshit." Finally, he pulled over and turned around to look at me in the eyes, directly, instead of in the rear-view mirror. As if this somehow gave him a better view of my real self.

"Look, young lady, I'm not sure what your deal is here but I'm having a hard time believing your story. I know that bus you jumped off left not far from where you're asking me to take you, so don't try to bullshit me anymore."

I opened my mouth to say—I had no idea what. He gave me a look and I closed my mouth and kept quiet.

"You're going to have to give me some kind of a deposit. At least for how much you owe me so far."

The meter was already over $30. I'd never racked up such a high cab fare. How much more would it be? How much of a beating was Marvin going to give me? Maybe I'd made the wrong choice. No way could I face Vivian. Marvin at least knew I could earn that back...

"Well?"

"I don't have that money, but please don't call the cops. I have a rich boyfriend. He'll pay the bill no problem when we get there. Please don't call the cops. It's because of them that I got this." I held up my arm.

"What, not horseback riding?"

"I wish." I looked down at my lap, traced the edge of my cast with my finger. Hoped he'd feel sorry for me. Normally I hated the thought of anyone having pity for me but I needed this ride... home. My new home. Old home was... not something I could face.

He let out a long, heavy sigh, deciding. "If he's NOT there or CAN'T pay, then I *will* call the cops and I don't care how many more horseback riding accidents you have, understand?"

"Yes, I understand."

"Okay, let's go then." He pulled back into traffic.

I just hoped when we got there I could actually *find* Marvin. He'd been out more and more, both physically and mentally. Too much weed, I figured.

The bus ride away from Port Authority took forever, but the cab ride back somehow seemed longer, as I watched those red numbers on the cab's meter tick higher and higher. I didn't think he'd take the long way around, like cab drivers did sometimes, because that was more money he might not get if he did have to call the cops on me.

By the time we pulled up to Marvin's hotel, the meter was over $80. I was in big trouble if I couldn't pay it, and maybe beat to shit if Marvin did pay it. Before the car came to a complete stop, I said, "Be right back," and jumped out, leaving the door open. It was long past midnight by now so Marvin could've been at a club, at a friend's house, who knew? The elevator took forever, the ding on each floor sounded loud in the empty, dark night.

The key from my purse, next to that little address book I should've ditched long ago, didn't want to work. My hand shook. The door flung open, key still in the lock.

Marvin's towering figure loomed over me. I couldn't read his face. Not quite awake? I burst into tears. Didn't realize I'd been holding them in. Holding my breath. He hugged me close.

"Hey, sweet girl, now why are you crying? What could be as bad as all that?" He bent down, and held my face in his hands, wiping away a tear with his large thumb.

"They... the cops..."

"Just breathe sweetheart. Are they after you?" He pulled me into the room and closed the door quietly.

"No, we have to go back out there. The cab driver needs money or he's going to call the cops."

His eyes went wide a second, they looked red. "Just outside?"

"Yeah."

We went back down to the curb where the cabby leaned on his car with his arms crossed. He looked Marvin up and down, and stood up in case he needed to fight or flee. The cabby tensed as Marvin reached behind him... and pulled out his wallet. The cabby let out a breath, and held out his hand.

"That'll be eighty bucks."

Marvin pulled a hundred out of the fat stack of bills in his wallet. Slapped the bill in the cabby's hand. "Keep the change." He turned on his fancy dress shoe heel and put his arm around me.

The cabby looked right at me before I turned away with Marvin. I couldn't quite read his expression either. Like he'd swallowed something bad-tasting. He shoved the bill in his pocket and left.

"You ok, darlin'?" Marvin brushed my cheek again.

I nodded.

"Now, how'd you get so far out of the city? Eighty dollars away?" His sweet voice had a hint of anger in it, when he said *eighty dollars*. "And what happened to your money?" I didn't tell him the whole story, including the address book I wasn't supposed to have.

"I came back to you," I said over and over. "Because I *know* you *love* me."

Chapter Fourteen

Shoes Not Made for Walking

Compared to Buffalo, the streets of Manhattan sometimes didn't seem real. Everything louder. Bigger. Like another country. Like something out of a movie, especially when I would see a movie and spot something familiar. Rockefeller Center! Ice Skaters! Broadway! As far as the school of hard knocks goes, New York provided so much to learn, with so many people speaking different languages, in their different body types, different skin types and textures.

I liked to look at all the different kinds of clothes, especially the shoes. I'd glance at them when passing by the glittering shop windows in the Fashion District, the times I ventured those few blocks away from where I usually worked those first years. Stayed closer to 42nd street most of the time. I'd gotten used to the noise of the buses coming and going, people yelling, even the smell. Diesel mixed with pee.

The other girls wore those impossibly high and over-exaggerated heels. Like something out of a circus act, like they were acrobats, balancing while walking. They caught me looking, then noticed my shoes, too. The worn-out flats I'd brought from Buffalo had a little break while I was in Rikers. I'd worn through the edge on my right-pinky toe side, and the left was about to poke through. They noticed my shoes too.

"Hey chica," one of them said to me one night when I was too tired to stay away from them. They usually traveled in small packs. I'd been flying solo. Two others lingered nearby, snapping their gum and looking me up and down, half watching the traffic going by for potential customers.

"Hey, I'm talking to you," the tallest and meanest-looking one said. I touched the blade tucked under my bra and gave her a hard look, not wanting a fight but not afraid to fight back, if needed. I missed the cast that Marvin had kindly pulled off for me, possibly a little too early.

"Por que tiene those fucked-up shoes?"

I glanced down at the worn-out but comfortable flats, then at her expensive-looking heels, black with rhinestone accents. They were beautiful. Probably not comfortable.

One of the three girls, wearing fire-engine red stilettos, chimed in when I didn't answer and didn't look up. This was my second of two shifts. I was too tired to defend myself from this verbal harassment. I told myself, *Sticks and stones*, but sometimes this kind of assault felt worse. I'd gotten used to the whacks from customers or Marvin when he got mad. And Marvin always had a reason, he'd explain to me all his reasons and even talk about how we'd have a baby together, to *show*

how he really loved me. I liked the idea of having a baby but didn't know if I could. Maybe he'd hit me less if I was pregnant.

"Yah, how come you wear los mismo zapatos, every day?"

They spoke Spanglish, sliding between English and Spanish or Portuguese sometimes mid-sentence.

Before I dropped out of high school, I didn't always pay attention in language class. Somehow hearing it on the street was easier to pick up. Part out of necessity, for words like feletta (knife), pistola or cuerte for gun. Zapato, for shoe, stuck in my mind because it sounded a little like zap-a-toe. If I could've zapped my little sticking-out baby toe at that moment, I would've made it disappear. Maybe into some beautiful new ruby slippers so I could click my heels together three times and be home, take my shoes off, and sleep.

"Estupida," said the first when I didn't respond.

"Ella no se nada." *She doesn't know anything*, said red-stiletto girl.

The third one wore these plain black shoes with a modest heel and strap across the top. Almost like Mary Janes. A lot like those jazz shoes I'd see on the performers there on Broadway, those rare stolen afternoons when I'd spend a few bucks on the cheap, last-minute tickets you could buy from those special booths, sometimes set up on a median strip or shoved between the street vendors. I'd listen to the music, look at the elaborately made-up faces, watch the skirts twirl and be transported for a too-short hour or two. I'd remember what the girl on the bus back from Rikers had said, that I wanted to believe so badly, about how I could be a star. Before she stole all my money.

Had this hooker stolen her shoes from a dancer? Borrowed them from a sister? I glanced up at her face for a moment to see if it told a story. Her eyes looked tired and showed heartbreak. I bet she had once been a dancer. Didn't work out. Of course not.

She caught my glance a moment, then flashed a look of pity.

"Vamanos," she said to the other two. Maybe she was the leader after all, not the black-rhinestoned shoe girl. I knew how important it was to figure these things out, especially when outnumbered, but I hadn't yet mastered the art. "Leave her alone, she's just a kid."

As they wandered away, chattering and yelling things at passing cars, I let out a deep breath, noticing how sore my feet were. I'd held on too long to the well-broken-in shoes my Nana had bought for me, what felt like forever ago, to wear to school.

I left my corner early, full of a new resolve, and went straight home to Marvin. Too bad if he hit me. I was already in pain. I threw the cash I'd earned that night right at him.

"What's with you, girl?" he asked, half smiling, maybe at all the money, maybe at my silly pout.

"I can't work two eight-hour shifts every single night!" I yelled with a voice that had been boiling since I saw the girl in the dancing shoes and her pity, which I hated more than insults.

He counted the money, so many bills. "You did good tonight. Shit, girl, it's okay. Come here." He put on his kind eyes. The deep-brown, twinkly eyes that first drew me into him, like quicksand, what seemed like so long ago now.

"My feet hurt!" My voice came out a little softer.

"Okay, sweetheart," he touched my back and I melted into the warmth of his hand. Desperate for a sympathetic voice, for something familiar. "You keep making money like this and you can skip the second shift." He must've known something had happened out there. Something inside of me had broken down, like my old shoes. He knew he'd reach a limit.

Normally I'd be afraid of what he'd say or do if I didn't just go along with whatever he wanted. But now I didn't have to work the second shift. Now he rubbed my back with that warm, gentle touch that made everything hurt less. He did love me, after all.

"And I want new shoes." It started as a demand, but came out more like a question.

"Any shoes you want, girl. Any shoes you want."

I played that scene over in my head that night as I fell asleep, and dreamed of the new shoes I'd pick.

Chapter Fifteen

The Golden Rule is Bullshit

My Nana always told us kids how to act right. She's the one who taught me the golden rule about "Do unto others as you'd have them do unto you." I didn't understand all the "done unto" fancy wording so she tried again: "Treat other people how you'd like to be treated." I wanted to say, "I'd like to be treated to some ice cream," but Nana had also taught me not to sass too much. No one likes a wise ass.

Her lessons on how to treat people swirled through my head the first time I met a disabled person—a kid back in junior high who showed up one day at school in a wheelchair. There was something wrong with his hands and his neck, too, like it took some effort for him to lift his head and see what was going on around him. Or maybe he just didn't want to look.

Some of the other kids were ruthless, not usually to his face, because when he looked at you out of his big brown eyes, they seemed to say, "You should be glad you're not me."

That kid was around for a couple weeks, then gone. Someone said they took him to a school that specialized in people like him. Whatever that meant. Little did I know that later I'd specialize in people like him. No one else wanted to. It started with Sam, in New York City.

Sam didn't have a wheelchair, just these cane things attached to his arms for balance, since his limbs didn't work quite right. He didn't have as many problems as the kid back in school, just the thing with his legs, and he didn't talk so good. It took him a while to get words out. But I could tell when he saw me he was happy I stopped in front of him, and when I looked right at him, he smiled awkwardly, his grin not exactly symmetrical.

"You're not going to ignore me like everyone else?" A little bit of spittle came out of the side of his mouth as he said this.

"*I'm* not going to ignore you, why would I do that?"

"Most people ignore me."

"Well," I said, putting a hand on his arm, partially trying to steady him, partly to be flirty, "I'm not most people."

His eyes went wide, especially when I bent down a little so he could see some cleavage.

"Did you want a date?"

He nodded.

"Do you have some money?"

He nodded again.

"Come with me." With him I didn't have to worry he might be an undercover cop. Or someone who'd beat me up later.

When we got up the stairs, he refused any assistance and was obviously annoyed, so I never did that again. I just negotiated a price and got payment up front, as I was taught. He paid me in 20s, which took a while for him to extract from his pocket, one at a time, his hand trembling. I wanted to offer to help him, but I didn't want to insult him again.

Later, he asked me if he could see me again, and the next time he pulled one wrinkled and abused $5 bill out of his pocket, then another, one at a time, in what would become his standard M.O. because he figured out that I didn't start the clock ticking until after he paid me. And the whole time he was paying me, I talked to him and let him look at my cleavage, which wasn't much but he liked it.

"Fives again," I said, the second time he brought them. I tried to keep my tone flirty and not annoyed. He was very smart, and had a funny grin as he slowly pulled each bill out. But I wanted him to know that I was on to him.

"Yeah, I like Lincoln," he said to explain the fives.

"I like *all* the presidents," I joked. I wondered how many conversations he had a week, if everyone ignored him. Maybe his only conversations were with people he bought things from. I hoped he had a family that loved him, but I didn't want to feel sorry for him, didn't want to feel pity, and mostly I didn't want to think about what nastiness might be on that floor under him when he flopped down on it. He insisted on taking off his jeans and shirt, skipping the sheet-covered, plywood beds. It was foggy out, and the blue neon of a flashing sign outside made his skin a weird bluish-gray, like he was from another planet. Or already dead.

I asked him if he wanted to lie on the bed, which wasn't more comfortable, but at least the sheet was washed every now and then. The sticky, uneven, littered with who-knew-what floor may never have been washed. You couldn't even tell what color the linoleum used to be. Yellow? Brown? Grey? There was some kind of square pattern visible, here and there where the nasty gunk was less thick.

Besides all the small bills, he also brought a pair of spike heels in a duffle bag. The shoes and new clothes I'd gotten after that one brave moment with Marvin were cute but not spiky like Sam brought, after he'd worked up some courage. He liked the kind most of the other girls wore every day that to me screamed *hooker* and were really uncomfortable, 5-inch red ones I could barely stand in, never mind walk. Luckily, I only needed to wear them long enough to press a heel into his super-pale skin. This is what he liked. He said something about how the pain made him feel alive.

After we'd done this a few times and he felt more comfortable telling me exactly what he wanted, he'd yell "Harder, harder!"

Someone listening from one of the other rooms might think it was just regular sex happening. You might think I'd be glad that I didn't even have to take off my clothes to make Sam happy. He should've been an ideal customer. But eventually I couldn't do it anymore. He wanted me to put my full weight on him, press as hard as possible.

I'd dealt with customers who liked pain, but this was extreme. I couldn't grind his testicles like that, I just couldn't do it, no matter how much he said he liked it, no matter how many more Lincolns he promised to give me. I just couldn't stand to see him in all that pain. He'd suffered enough already.

Nana was wrong about *do unto others as they'd have done unto them* because some people like some pretty fucked up stuff done unto them.

The last time I saw him, I kissed him on the cheek and looked him in the eyes. "You deserve to be happy, Sam," I said. His eyes filled with tears.

"Please don't go," he begged.

"I can't make you happy." I touched his arm one last time and walked away.

Chapter Sixteen

Mariposa and Cherry

I'd gotten better at keeping Marvin happy. This was mostly about not getting into trouble and bringing him more and more money as I got faster at my job. He had additional girls working for him, too, and we could all see that he spent a lot on fancy clothes and jewelry and pot. He had less time for me, and I didn't feel so much like his special girl anymore, but that was kind of okay, because I didn't really like being around him that much anymore.

So one day when he asked, "How'd you like to go to Montreal with Mariposa? Check out the scene up there?"

I said "Sure."

Mariposa, of course not her real name, had been in the game longer than me but didn't seem as mean as most. I was a fresh turn-out compared to her, in spite of all I'd learned and been through already.

During our all-day bus ride to Montreal, she tried to teach me everything she knew, way more than Sheri ever did for me, especially about how to get set up in a new city.

When we got off the bus in Montreal, we found a place called Club 21, which looked okay. Mariposa and I shrugged at each other then climbed up the stairs to check it out. The inside was pretty dark. That worked in our favor since people would be less likely to notice we were teenagers. The blue and purple neon around the edges of the room reminded me a little of the signs back on 42nd Street. We crossed the mostly empty dance floor to get to the bar, and the whole thing vibrated under our feet. We grabbed each other for balance and giggled at the fancy gimmick. I'd heard of vibrating beds, but never a whole vibrating dance floor.

At the bar, I did my best New-York-tough face, but just ordered a soda from the friendly female bartender. I could hear Marvin's warnings in my ears, "You better not get caught up again, I don't wanna have to find no Canadian lawyer."

Mariposa nudged me and pointed, "Do those sofas look like dicks to you?"

"A little," I replied. "I don't see any actual dudes in this place, do you?"

She'd noticed the furniture but not the people. So much for having more experience than me.

"Oh shit." She started giggling again. "Is this a girls only... gay place or something?"

I shrugged. "Oops."

Then I remembered my promise to call Marvin when we got there. I found a pay phone and told him about Club 21. I thought he might find it funny, too. He used to like to laugh and joke.

Instead, he yelled so loud I pulled the phone away from my ear. "Bitch, you better never go back in there."

We didn't go in there, and the next couple of bars were also a bust so we didn't stick around long. On the bus ride home, Mariposa and I didn't talk so I had time to think about what the kind bartender at Club 21 had said to me as she took my empty glass away. She'd looked me up and down, squinted at me a bit and told me, "You wouldn't look so young if you weren't chewing gum."

I thought about what else I could do to not look so young. More makeup? Different hair?

I should've been thinking about going back home and going to the prom with all the other kids at school. Or, since prom wasn't really my thing, I could've been thinking of how to convince them to let me play on the boy's hockey team. I was a damn good goalie. Could block those slap shots like nobody's business. Who knew that taking smacks and whacks and having a good reaction time from all that hockey I'd played as a kid would later help me defend myself against the mean johns.

Those kids at school probably would have forgotten all about my shame and moved on to someone else's troubles. But I was just a kid. And a people-pleaser. Didn't know better. Marvin was the person I needed to please. That's what I knew.

After the Montreal fuck-up, Marvin decided Mariposa was a little too green or maybe we just had too much fun or something, so instead he sent me out with Cherry. This time we were headed for Atlantic City. And by now the seasons had changed and the weather there was freezing-ass cold.

From the bus station, we got a cab driver to take us to the busiest part of the boardwalk. "You know," Cherry said to the cab driver, using her Georgia drawl, "the spot where ya got the most tourists. Know what I mean, darlin'?"

The cab driver drove us right up to a couple of uniformed cops. The fucker! We ducked behind the driver's seat, not wanting those cops to see us, but then he explained the drill. As long as we stayed in a designated area and paid them their "lunch money"—that's what he called it—they'd leave us alone.

We thanked the cabby and paid the cops for some pretty expensive lunches. Then they pointed in the direction of the street for girls like us, and we were off and running. Much better than the Club 21 incident.

Better, until one early morning a few weeks in. I'll never forget. The wind made the temperature drop even more. Cherry stood next to me, her teeth chattering louder than mine, while we waited for the morning sun to creep across the ocean over to us.

We could no longer stand and wait on the boardwalk or inside the casino, because security would kick us out or bust us for loitering. The nice cab driver had warned us about that too. We waited and waited in the cold, all the time talking about how nice the sun's warmth would feel on our skin. We'd both worked the night shift, two blocks over from Caesar's Palace, and made a ton of money, but hoped to make a little more before calling it a night. That way we could enjoy the beach and boardwalk and sun, with some cash left held back from what we wired to Marvin.

Cherry wore leopard short-shorts—skin tight—a brown silk blouse with a plunging vee, no bra. She said it worked to give the johns a peek and maybe even a "quick feel to seal the deal." She stood on five-inch block-heeled boots that clopped when she walked. She claimed men liked taller women. Her perfect skin made even me want to touch it.

Around her neck hung a doubled string of cheap amber beads that swung down between her breasts.

I had a little more meat on me and was a few months older, so I felt kinda responsible for her, even though she seemed to know what she was doing, or at least acted like it.

I took off the London Fog, fur-lined coat I'd grabbed off a john, and wrapped it around Cherry. He hadn't tipped me and was yelling insults as the cab driver drove away, slow enough that I jerked the coat right out the passenger window. I intended to hock it as soon as I had the chance. But for that freezing moment just before the sun came up that promising day, I could see she needed it more.

But, she shoved it away. "No, no, I'm not taking your charity. You're as cold as I am and it's your coat."

"We'll share it. You get it for five minutes then I'll take a turn."

"I'll rent it from you. I ain't takin' none o' ya charity."

"I won't take your money." I insisted. Not sure which of us was more stubborn.

"Okay, how about we both get in the coat. It's almost big enough." Cherry giggled.

"Really? You think we'll fit?"

"Hell, yes. Come on. Snuggle up."

She slipped into one sleeve, put her arm around my waist, and instantly warmed up. We faced each other to get the coat buttoned, her breath warm and sweet—peppermint salt water taffy, her favorite flavor. A child living in a degenerate adult world who kept candy in her purse. I missed the gum I'd quit chewing after Montreal.

Cherry giggled again. "'Two peas in a pod,' my mama used to say." She was sad all of a sudden, the dawning sun causing her face to look older without its usual smile perking everything up. I wanted to ask about her mom, but didn't want to talk about mine, so I just echoed what she said.

"Yup, two peas. And now I have to pee. Bladder like a pea. I can't stop saying P."

That made her giggle again. It was nice to make someone laugh. Like how Vivian and I used to make each other laugh. I missed her. I missed the closeness.

Cherry said, "I could eat a horse. Let's hobble down the street to the White Castle, they're open 24 hours. We can buy a sack full of them cute little burgers."

"You mean like this? Bound up in this...this pea pod?"

She reached around, pinched me on my ass, and giggled. "Hell yeah, like this. This is fun." Her flowing hair brushed up against my cheek. She moved her hand from around my waist up to my mouth and popped in a peppermint salt water taffy. Her finger lingered on my lip. It tasted sooo sweet, almost too sweet, making my teeth hurt. Or maybe that was just the cold. But I wouldn't spit it out. We started shuffling down the sidewalk laughing and poking each other. I needed a friend, but never thought I'd find one here on the streets, working.

As we reached White Castle, three punk gangsters not old enough to run with the older set, rode their probably-stolen peddle bikes down the street headed right toward us. Gold jewelry hung around their necks and twinkled on their fingers. Pure punk.

I figured we'd avoid them by slipping through the restaurant's door. We unbuttoned the jacket and slid out into the air, still so cold it freckled my arms and legs with chicken skin. I shivered and folded the coat over my arm and opened the door.

The three boys laid their bikes to the side, skidding to a stop in front of us. Young boys with bikes. Damn punks. They laughed and chided us like they usually do, too scared to make an offer. Not that I would oblige them. I wouldn't. But they grew nasty.

One of the smaller ones called us, "Putas." He took change out of his pocket and flung it, the coins pelting us and clattering to the ground. Mostly pennies. Beside me, Cherry started to reach down into her boot for a pearl-handled switchblade, a real one, a Stiletto, not one of the knock-offs found most often on the street. Real steel, not easy to break. I put my hand on her arm to stop her. The boy was just posturing, probably thinking this was how a man was supposed to act. What did he know? Who did he have for a role model but other street thugs.

Too late, the little one saw her aggressive move. He puffed up his chest and charged her. "What 'cha gonna do, huh bitch? You gonna do something? What cha got there? You got a knife? You gonna stick me?" Cherry spit in his face. Enraged, he pulled back a fist to slug her—to slug my friend. I kicked him in the chest. He fell on his back gasping, arms waving, a turtle unable to turn over.

I grabbed Cherry's arm and we ran into the restaurant. She continued yelling filthy words at them, words a young girl shouldn't know. The door closed. We laughed with relief.

Princesses live in castles. We were princesses of the street. We used the money we'd earned hours before to sit and eat and talk about our futures. Cherry was saving her money to buy a car. She didn't like the cold months in New Jersey and would drive to California, to Hollywood. Give up her street life and get a job as a waitress, or a movie producer or writer. Maybe even a movie star. She flicked her hair over her shoulder to demonstrate.

I loved her dream and would have happily joined her in it, but I had already taken too large a bite out of the real world, not the fantasy one she believed in, and that taste was bitter. I nodded and said, "Oh, yes, that would be great," in all the right places. Sad for her and at the same time, I regretted my own loss of innocence.

After an hour, I told her I had to get some sleep.

Her dream, the one she told with such excitement, rattled around in my head. Could such a dream really come true?

As we walked out of the restaurant, I put the coat on Cherry and took in the beautiful colors of the sky. Breathed in the salt-scented air. The beaches in California were supposed to be even more beautiful and not so cold.

I turned to face Cherry, and my breath caught in my throat as I tried to scream. Little Junior was running up on her from behind, the blade in his hand reflecting the sun now higher in the morning sky. I started to pull her back just as the scream broke loose from my lungs. "Cherry!" She turned and froze, her eyes huge, an innocent baby doe seeing death approach.

She dropped the bag of extra White Castle Burgers. Urine ran down her leg to the sidewalk. Little Junior collided into her, buried the knife deep in her chest. I continued to yell as I heard a grunt, the last sound Cherry ever made. Like someone kicking a metal drum.

My friend Cherry wilted to the ground, blood pumping from her chest, puddling on the sidewalk. She lay in her own blood and urine, staring up at me but not seeing.

Tears wet my face. I sobbed, looking around for someone to help. I couldn't deal with this. My friend had died right in front of me on the sidewalk. I turned to the White Castle hamburger joint. No knights came riding out on white horses to save the fair maidens.

It was just me in the cold, Cherry's blood soaking into the fur lining of my coat.

Chapter Seventeen

Paradise Found

In the cheap motel room Cherry and I shared, I called Marvin and told him everything, hardly stopping to breathe. I wasn't asking for permission to leave. I just told him I was out of there. The main thing he cared about was whether or not the cops thought I had something to do with the murder or if they were going to need me to testify or anything. "I dunno," I repeated a couple of times. "That could have been me, you know."

"I know, Babe. Come home."

"That almost was me. Coulda been me." How was it fair that I'd survived that stabbing in New York, but Cherry didn't survive? Could I have done something more to save her? I shook the bad thoughts out of my head. Had to keep moving, had to get back.

When I stepped out of the motel for the last time, a gust of cold wind hit me. I thought of the warm fur coat, and paused. What did I do with it? Then I remembered the pool of blood, and how I'd covered Cherry with it there on the sidewalk. Stupid. She didn't need a coat.

She didn't want it anyway. Now I might freeze to death, and we'd both be dead.

On the long bus ride home, I dozed off a few times, but the bouncing of the bus caused my head to knock on the cold window, jarring me back awake. Or the memory of what had happened flashed in my head, making my eyes pop open. Felt like it just happened. Or that it didn't happen at all, like I'd seen it in a movie or heard about it from someone else. I remembered the look in her eyes as she left the world. No California for me? No Hollywood? I thought about going to Hollywood myself, to live out her dream. But that place might be even worse. At least I knew what to expect in New York. From Marvin.

He didn't say much to me when I got back. Just looked at me a little differently.

His other girls asked me about Atlantic City, all huddled around, like I was so special, so lucky I got to go somewhere new. I glanced at him. He shook his head. No words needed for me to hear him tell me: Don't say a fuckin' word about what happened to Cherry.

"Cold," I offered. They wanted more details. *At least she had dreams, plans to get out.* Maybe it *should* have been me instead of her. Could I have helped her get out? Maybe if we both fled together?

"Where's Cherry?"

I held down tears, looking at the floor to avoid anyone's stare.

"She's ... going to stay there a while longer."

I didn't know what would actually happen to her body. Would anyone claim it? Would someone come from Georgia to identify her and bring her home? I'd heard about a place in New York with unmarked graves. ... I needed to think of something else.

"Yes," Marvin clapped his hands together, "and the rest of you need to get back out there." He sounded a little kinder than normal. Like he was a basketball coach, not a pimp. Go team! Rebounds, get those rebounds!

Marvin did pay extra attention to me, probably worried I was broken somehow. I was. My *heart* was broken. He talked about us having a baby again. I figured that's partly how he kept the other girls tied to him, but I didn't care about not being that special. At least someone cared enough to take me to a doctor to have me checked out. More than one doctor, when the first one told me I couldn't have kids, I couldn't hold my tears in anymore. "Don't worry baby, we'll get you all fixed up," he told me, and took me to another doctor for another opinion until he found one who finally said, "Sure, there's a small chance it's possible." I wondered, though. Did the guy just say because he was afraid of Marvin?

A few months later, Marvin decided to send me to Las Vegas, by myself this time. They had slot machines everywhere. Worse than Atlantic City. Even in the airport. I got distracted by all the pretty colors and flashing lights and promises of huge payouts. As if I could win my fortune and never have to work again, if I just got lucky.

When I finally called, and Marvin chewed me out over the phone for not making hardly any money, I told him there was too much competition. Hotel rooms were expensive. The pimps were big and mean and so were the cops, and none of them looked the other way like the ones in Atlantic City. All of this was true, but mostly I didn't want to figure it out all over again, in this city that made no sense. In the middle of the desert. Nothing around. Just crime and gambling everywhere. Depressing.

He let me come home. Besides a few road trips, when he came along with a few other girls, the traveling slowed down for a few years.

I wasn't a teenager anymore, and he wasn't getting any younger either. He rationalized that our best earning potential was right there in New York. Or could he sense I was tiring of him and the scene?

One night as I handed him his money, he touched me on the cheek, grinning more than normal. His eyes looked more glassy than usual.

"Maria, babe, I got a good one for you."

Good one, what? I didn't ask. John? Joke? When was the last time he told a joke?

"How'd you like to go to ..."

I closed my eyes and tried not to wince. When I opened them again, he said:

"Hawaii!" He made some awkward hand motions—like the hula?

"Really?" Hawaii was supposed to be paradise. When I watched game shows as a kid, lots of times the grand prize, or what the winners said they wanted to do with their cash winnings, was to go to Hawaii. Besides, that was far away from Marvin, as far away from him as I could get and still be in the states. So I was glad to go.

As the plane flew closer, I looked out the window at all the ocean. It went on forever. So much blue ... and white fluffy clouds, like heaven. Most maps of the United States showed Hawaii and Alaska in little cut-outs right next to the other 48 states. The in-flight magazine showed a big world map with the real spacing, all the flights from cities all over the U.S. to Hawaii. The tiny islands were just as far from the West Coast as the West Coast was from New York. So much blue and nothing—Hawaii looking so small in the middle of the Pacific. Out the window stretched blue and more blue for miles and miles with an occasional boat.

In the distance, the soft slope where the earth was definitely round like a huge beach ball. I thought of the line about Columbus, who "sailed the ocean blue" and didn't fall off.

When the pilot finally announced we'd be able to see some land out the window, it didn't look real. Where were all the buildings? So much green and the white sand beaches with white caps on the waves. Everything looked so bright. I needed sunglasses. The blue of the ocean looked bluer somehow than any blue I'd ever seen. Like the glass in a marble with slivers of aqua and green.

We turned on the final approach into Honolulu, and I saw some tiny buildings but not that many, just scattered here and there with Diamond Head Crater in the distance like you see on the ads for Hawaii, or a poster, not an actual place.

The pilot told us we were going to land on the reef runway, and I wasn't sure what that meant, but it looked as if we were about to land right on the ocean. Part of me wanted to warn the stewardesses. "Hey, we're about to land on the ocean!" But what did I know? There was that TV show *Fantasy Island*, with the little guy yelling, "De plane, de plane!" just before the airplane actually DID land right on the water. Besides, I was too busy looking at the ocean, and all the boats, even surfers on that super blue-turquoise ocean. At the last second, some land showed up under us and we bounced a little when the wheels touched. Everyone cheered.

As soon as I stepped onto the stairway they'd rolled up to the door, the air felt different. Warm and muggy. Humid. Like a hug. The whole place smelled of flowers. I learned later it was the plumeria leis that had such a strong smell. This muggy place was also very huggy! On the tarmac, local people returning home had friends and family members loading them up with leis and hugs and kisses. Even some of the visitors were greeted by people with signs baring their name. A couple of different tour groups were greeted by these beautiful hula girls, with caramel skin and long dark hair, wearing only a bikini top and a grass skirt or sarong wrapped around their hips.

For a second, I wondered if someone would come up and give me a lei, but then I snapped back to reality. No way Marvin would have paid any extra for some fancy flower lei greeting. I could hear him in my head saying, "You're supposed to take their money to get laid, not get lei'd yourself!" Not that he joked around much anymore. At least I could still make my own little jokes.

I followed the crowd outside the terminal to the Wiki-Wiki bus, which took us to baggage claim. The blue sky and the palm trees swaying in the trade winds looked like a movie, and in the cozy bus the scent of the leis was almost overwhelming. Most were yellow plumeria, some pink. Others were made of carnations in one solid fat lei the width of my fist, or with single carnations in different colors, alternating with also fragrant tuba roses which were white and like a cross between a rose and a plumeria. A hula girl explained about all the different kinds, and how long they'd last, and where the flowers were grown and who made them. Felt like I was back in school again, learning lessons. For a second my eyes filled with tears. I missed school and my teachers, so curious about everything. Was it too late for me to go back? I took a deep breath of flower-scented air. Needed to focus on getting a room and a cab and the lay of the land.

While I waited for the bags to show up, I checked out the variety of people waiting with me. Lots of Asians. Always my favorite potential clients, especially the non-Yakuza Japanese. I soon learned the white people being greeted were called "haole" here, sometimes "fuckin' haole" or "fuckin' mainland haole." Especially if the mainlander said something stupid like, "Well, back in the STATES, we have...."

I didn't see a single black person in the whole baggage claim area or airport.

A large display with the label Hotels stood next to the sliding glass doors to the street. Back-lit ads, about the size of notecards, showed the names and logos for dozens of hotels. I had no idea which one to pick. Marvin told me to go to Waikiki. I figured the one called the Waikikian was probably close to Waikiki, so I picked up the phone on the display and asked the nice lady who answered if they had any vacancies, and they did. So far so good.

Outside I got a cab. The driver seemed friendly enough, asking if it was my first time in Hawaii, and what New York was like. When we got to the Waikikian, I pulled out my cash to pay him.

"Hey, where do the girls work?" I asked.

He looked in my eyes for a second, then down at the money in my hand. I thought he might ask me, "What's a nice girl like you asking a question like that?" or try to claim he didn't know the answer. Like most people, he just wanted the money and not my reasons for asking.

"Mostly on Kuhio," he said, "one street over, a couple blocks down."

"Thanks." I handed him the money, with a nice tip, for his help.

"Mahalo," he replied. "Good luck." He drove off.

The lobby of the Waikikian looked like the inside of a very large grass hut with lots of tikis. The people were so friendly. Even the giant security guard greeted me with "Aloha," and a warm smile. He really meant it.

"Aloha to you, too," I replied in my most grown-up, I-know-what-I'm-doing voice. He was the kind of big bouncer-type I could use on my team. That is, if he didn't mind how I planned to use this hotel for my home and office. Most security guards caught on quick. I needed to make him my friend, right away.

"Aloha, welcome to the Waikikian." The woman at the front desk wore the fanciest muumuu I'd ever seen. Not like the little house dresses my Nana used to wear that looked more like pajamas or maternity dresses. This woman's floral print dress was fitted in the middle with tons of ruffles along the top like a permanent, built-in lei. She also had a real plumeria lei that sat on top of her head like a halo. "How can I help?" she asked.

I thought, *Just some keys to my own piece of this heaven*. I said, "Two rooms, please."

"Adjoining?"

"No, as separate as possible, if you can." I'd pick which one made the most sense for my office and use the other one for home.

"No problem. And how many nights?"

I gave her a cash deposit for the first week and told her it might be longer.

As soon as I got to the room, I pulled off my sweater and pants that smelled like cigarette smoke from the airplane and pulled on my bikini. Back in New York City, to get any kind of tan at all, you had to go up on top of a building and hope to get a few sunbeams peaking through the haze in between the other skyscrapers. And then there were always people from the other buildings who could see. One guy always stood right next to the window of his big fancy apartment, wackin' himself off for anyone to see, when I wished he would've just watched porn on the cable on his big TV.

But now all that nastiness was behind me. Maybe even Marvin, too.

My ground-floor room was so sunny and bright, with pictures of flowers, floral-print everything. The hotel room sliding glass door led directly to the outside. I opened the door and was hit again by the muggy warm air and the bright sunlight. My eyes adjusted enough for me to spot a sign that said BEACH, framed by a couple of tikis, with an arrow to the right. So much different than all the neon and giant billboards in New York. The cab driver had mentioned how billboards were illegal in Hawaii. Nothing but cute flowered signs and beautiful scenery in every direction.

The beach was right there, this huge bright carpet of sand, like they'd built the hotel on the beach. You could even rent a sailboat on the ocean. Waves crashed with soothing, rhythmic sounds as I walked along the edge of the water, cooling my feet from the hot sand. The hotel next door, the Ilikai, looked familiar. The cab driver had said it was featured in the opening credits of the original *Hawaii Five-O* TV show. But he didn't mention the huge lagoon behind it, the size of about half a football field, with a cute island in the middle of it. An island inside an island! This place did not seem real.

A couple of people attempted to windsurf on the flat calm surface of the lagoon, while little kids played at the edges where they wouldn't get knocked over by the ocean waves.

Just past that, a boat harbor with rows and rows of boats stretched off into the distance. "You see it in Gilligan's Island," I could hear the cab driver's voice in my head. "That's where they set sail for the 'tree-hour tour.'" I'd noticed he said "tree" instead of "three" and had an accent I'd only heard a few times before.

You could also rent a two-seater paddle boat that people paddled like a bicycle around the lagoon or in the ocean. That looked fun, but too much like work. I got myself one of those inflatable floaties. I planned to just relax in the sun and get some rays. The nice lady also tried to sell me some sunscreen. "'Cuz the rays mo' strong hea, Dea," she said, dropping the Rs at the end, with this accent I kept hearing.

Should've listened to her. Or not fallen asleep for so long under that warm caress of the muggy hug which would've gotten too hot, fast, if it wasn't for the fluffy white clouds drifting by for a touch of shade and the tradewinds like soft kisses, helping me nod off into the best sleep I'd had since I couldn't remember when.

I'd wake up for a second if a little kid shrieked with joy, then watch the people go by, or pick out animal shapes in the fluffy clouds, then drift off to sleep again.

I didn't even turn over to get my back. And when I did finally wake up, I couldn't quite open my eyes all the way, my face felt hot and puffy like I'd been smacked a bunch of times, and the rest of me felt oddly cold, like I had died, and my limbs were in a morgue.

I stood up slowly, woozy. Nauseous. Were those blisters on my arms? The cool air conditioning in the lobby felt good on my face but made me shiver. I tried to wrap my half-deflated floaty thing around me like a comforter to keep me warm. In the gift shop, I started to feel a little dizzy and held onto the shelf of sunscreen I should've used.

"Oh honey," the cashier hurried over to me, "you SOOO sunburned. You got sun poisoning." My brain tried to understand what that meant as she yelled at someone behind me. "Aye! Kimo! Try wait!" The busboy she'd stopped was headed home for the night and agreed to take me to "Queens."

For a second I thought the Hawaiian monarchs were in charge of medical care, or maybe the transvestites in this town were also the nurses. Or maybe I was a little delirious from the sun poisoning. Either way I had a lot to learn about this place. Queens was the name of a hospital on Kimo's way home. He dropped me off at the emergency room. They loaded me up with liquids until I finally had to pee. In the bathroom mirror I almost didn't recognize myself. My face looked like a beat-up tomato. The ugly, bloated cousin of Mr. Potato Head: Ms. Tomato Head. Too stupid to get out of the sun. How was I going to find any customers looking like this?

Crap. Customers. I hadn't called Marvin yet, and I had nothing good to tell him. Another wave of cold washed over me. Fear. He was going to smack my face into even worse shape when he found out.

Chapter Eighteen

Day Two in Paradise

The next morning when I woke up, I struggled to open my puffy eyes. And my skin felt too hot and too cold at the same time. I carefully rolled on my side and looked out the window. The pink and blue sky with cute puffy clouds made me feel instantly better. Hopeful. I wanted to be like one of those clouds. Light and free of any worries. Just floating in the sky. Somewhere a silver lining or an angel might be up there that I couldn't see. Maybe my Nana, happy to see me so far away from Marvin.

Oh shit, Marvin. I was supposed to call him as soon as I got to the hotel. How long ago was that?

I jumped up and pressed the numbers on the phone as fast as I could. The sun was up so it must've been daytime. The red numbers on the clock radio said 7:15. Was it earlier or later in New York? I had no idea.

After one ring, he answered with just one word, "Talk."

"Hi Marvin, it's me, Ma—"

The yelling started. "What the fuck, bitch!?"

I held the receiver away from my ear. Looked out the window. Tried to be calm like a cloud.

"Where the hell you been? Didn't I tell you to call me as soon as your skinny ass got there? Tell me where the fuck you are?"

"Yes, but I—"

"You betta tell me you makin' so much money you had no time." He sounded so mad. But also far away. I liked him better when he was far away.

"I was in the hospital."

"What!? How'd you end up there? You okay?"

For a second, he actually sounded worried. But was it about me? Or the money he wanted from me? I hoped my trip to the hospital would get me a little sympathy. But should I tell him it was for a *sunburn*? I could already hear him saying how he was going to make me feel a real burn... But he didn't know where I was exactly. And why should I tell him? So he could come here and smack me around? I looked outside at the cute clouds. I could hear birds in the distance. Happy, free. I could be like them. I was strong enough and smart enough to figure out how to get myself here and set up. My skin felt better already. I looked in the mirror. Less puffy. If I didn't have to send him my earnings, I could stay here forever. In paradise. Free like the clouds and the birds.

"Never mind, Marvin, I can take care of myself." I hung up, then stared at the phone. What had I just done? Chills from fear or from sun poisoning—maybe both—crawled up and down my back. I realized I was holding my breath. I let it out slowly, and counted to ten. Who told me about doing that? I couldn't remember. Maybe Nana had whispered it in my ear. I looked back out at the clouds. They were gone.

I couldn't believe what I'd just done. I didn't even tell him the name of the hotel, or when I'd be going to the Western Union to send his money. MY hard-earned money. But what if I . . . didn't? Would he find me? He'd planned to come out here too, at least for a little while, after I figured out how things worked, as he called it.

To calm myself down, I took a long walk. All of Waikiki was only a couple of miles long—from one end at the big Ala Moana Shopping Center and the three-hour tour harbor to the other end at the Honolulu Zoo. The area that the cab driver told me about was only part of that. As long as there weren't a lot of other girls—should be easy.

I got some supplies at one of the many ABC stores that seemed to be on every corner. I told myself I'd be fine. I didn't need Marvin. Right? No. Didn't.

I tried to take a nap, but tossed and turned trying to find a less-sunburned spot that didn't hurt. My left shoulder was a little less blistered than the right. I liked the coconut smell of the lotion I'd slathered on so thick it stuck to the sheets. Might've dozed off a little.

I watched the sun go down over Waikiki Beach. Loads of tourists taking pictures. The horizon had sail boats here and there. Dinner cruise boats. None of it seemed real. Maybe I'd actually died in the hospital and this was heaven. Everyone smiling. My stomach growling brought me back to reality. I had about enough cash for one more meal. That was it. Had to get to work.

I found a Denny's restaurant near where the cab driver told me the girls worked. Something comforting about the familiar place, which is pretty much the same in Vegas or New York or wherever. Same scent of pancakes and coffee. Slightly sticky menus. I sat at the end of the counter where I could watch and listen.

The broken English they spoke sometimes sounded like Canadians I knew. Instead of "Eh" or "Ay?" at the end of a sentence, here they'd say, "Yeah?" Seemed more festive or playful somehow. Happier.

I ordered a Grand Slam because I could do what I wanted. Order pancakes for dinner. Drown them in fake maple syrup. I'd had the real stuff before, growing up so close to Canada. This stuff at least poured faster. I was so hungry. I'd seen an IHOP at the other end of Waikiki. I liked the pancakes there better because IHOP had blueberry and strawberry syrup, too. So you can make designs with the different colors. Maybe I'd go there for breakfast. Or later that night, if I wanted. Midnight snack!

The restaurant was full of colorful people, lots of them strawberry colored like me from too much sun. Some military guys with their short haircuts. Families dressed in matching flower-print outfits like I saw for sale in the ABC stores. Locals like the servers who I could mostly understand. Outside the window I saw lots of Japanese tourists. They'd look inside, maybe have a peek at the menu in the window, but not many came in.

Back in New York, the Japanese were my favorite customers. Tended to be much more polite and not once had any of them hit me. Instead they bowed and said please and thank you. Had to watch out for Yakuza, though, the badass organized crime guys, tattooed from head to toe and everything in between. The tattoos and hard look in their eyes made them easy to spot, to avoid. Outside the Denny's, I didn't see any, just some Japanese families and businessmen. This was going to be so much easier than Vegas. Or Atlantic City. The memory of Cherry flashed in my mind. She would have loved this place. All the sunshine and smiling people. She might've grabbed one of those surfboards and paddled out into the beautiful blue water, shouting, "Come on, Maria, the water's great!"

I tried to push that thought out of my mind. The last of pancakes, soaking up the fake syrup, reminded me of that coat soaking up her blood. I wiped my fingers and tossed my napkin on the plate. In that evil city, where was Marvin? He didn't help any. I'd survived that on my own, so this island paradise—where I didn't even have to worry about gloves or coats—would be a cakewalk. Kicked off by pancakes. I paid my bill and got out of there, and headed back to the hotel.

The room at the Waikikian was easy to get to without going through the lobby, just a quick shortcut along the beach which had a nice sidewalk. Such a big difference from the Girls! Girls! Girls! setup near the Port Authority in New York.

Just after midnight, I'd already made enough to cover my expenses for weeks. Without having to worry about Marvin, I wouldn't even need to work every night. I might even take up surfing or...

"Who's that guy?" One of the other girls on the street, who'd actually been not exactly friendly to me, but also not chasing me away, had a look of... fear? Awe? As she asked the question to no one in particular.

I turned and there he was. As though just my thought of taking a night off had caused him to appear out of thin air.

Larger than life and at least a head taller than anyone else around, Marvin—right in the middle of Kalakau Avenue. He seemed to move in slow motion. Like in a movie, complete with the tail of his coat fluttering behind him. I blinked a few times to make sure I was really seeing this.

"That's Marvin," I said. The girl walked away quickly, like I should have done, but my feet didn't move. My whole body felt cold and frozen, stuck to the ground.

On one side of him was his brother, who'd taught Marvin the trade back in the day. Both of them had bloodshot eyes that made them look extra scary as they stepped up on the sidewalk in front of me.

I flinched as he got within arms' reach, expecting at least a smack. He looked left and right, as if to check for cops. Still not a word. Just that glassy stare.

"You found me!" I said, breaking the ice, with my best smile. Marvin just nodded slightly, still staring hard at me. "Here, I got your room at the Waikikian." I spoke quickly. "Where's your stuff?"

He lifted one of his gold-and-diamond-ring-covered hands and pointed a thumb toward a cab on the other side of the street.

He moved that same huge hand toward me. For a second I thought he was going to grab me by the neck. He touched the side of my face, his palm cool on my cheek.

"What happened to your face?" His voice was so low I almost didn't hear him. For a moment, he reminded me of the old Marvin, the one who first talked me into going to New York with him.

"I tried to tell you on the phone—" My brain spun, looking for words that would keep me out of trouble. "Before we got cut off. The phones aren't that great here."

He squinted harder at me, like he knew I was lying.

"Sun poisoning." I pulled up my sleeve and showed him the blisters on my arm. "But I'm okay. You must be tired after that long flight." I couldn't believe how fast he'd gotten here from New York. Silly of me to think he wouldn't come and find me.

Marvin let go of my face and pointed across the street, to a skinny girl on a bench. "Show her the ropes." He turned on one expensive heel and stepped back onto Kalakaua Avenue, ignoring the do-not-walk sign, stepping into traffic like he was invincible, with no doubt the cars would stop for him. Some had to break hard. No one dared yell or flip him off. His brother hurried to catch up as Marvin disappeared into the back of the cab.

I held in tears, crossed the street when the light changed, and sat down next to New Girl, but didn't say a word. She let out a heavy sigh and started to crack her knuckles one by one. I gave her a look and she stopped, the fear in her eyes too similar to how she looked at Marvin. She switched to biting her already nubby nails. So much for surfing and days off.

I looked up to the sky, but it was too dark to see the clouds.

After Marvin left for the hotel, lots of emotions swirled around. Anger at myself for... what? Not hiding better? Maybe I wanted him to come. I did still love him, didn't I? Seeing New Girl did make me jealous. She was younger and thinner than me. A cute tiny, turned-up nose. Did Marvin like her more? She smiled at me when she caught me looking. Eyes tired but still innocent and sweet. Part of me wanted to tell her to run, get out while she could. This was no life for a young girl. What happened to her dreams?

I was surprised by my sudden maternal instinct. A bigger part of me didn't want to know or get too attached like I was with Cherry. I had to protect myself if I was going to survive in this business. And what else could I do? I had no other skills or training or even a high school diploma. Besides, Marvin wasn't THAT bad, compared to some of my mom's men.

"It's so warm here," New Girl said. She held her thin, bare arms out in front of her. "Almost like the air... just isn't there at all!" She looked at me with big, excited eyes. I knew what she meant, the air in New York often felt like it bit you. Painful cold. This air was more like a soft caress.

I nodded, and looked in the direction of the beach, a couple streets over." Just be careful in the sun here. It can turn you into Mr. Potato Head real fast."

"Mr. Potato?" she looked confused. I was about to ask her if she'd never seen Mr. Potato Head, but I didn't really want to know.

"Never mind, we gotta get to work."

She nodded, her smile gone.

"One good thing about the warm weather," I said, "fewer pockets to hide a wallet in."

She looked confused. "Fewer pockets?"

"Don't you ever... help yourself to a bigger tip?"

She tilted her head like a dog who'd just heard a strange sound. "You mean steal?"

I laughed. The way she sounded so surprised and horrified at the thought of breaking the law made me chuckle.

She looked around as if to see if anyone was listening in on our conversation.

"No? Not stealing?" she asked. "I don't know what you —"

"Listen, mija." I moved right up against her, getting in her face while I lifted the contents of her pocket on the side next to me. "You've gotta learn."

She pulled her head back, eyes wide. I felt bad that I scared her, then noticed the soft texture of what I'd snagged from her pocket. I held it out between us. A rabbit's foot.

"Hey, I have one just like that." Her smile returned for just a second, then confusion. "Wait," she touched her pocket, "how did you do that?"

Now she looked like a kid at a magic show, and I'd just pulled a live rabbit from a hat. The thought of what happened to the rest of this rabbit made me drop the freaky thing. It fell between the slats of the bench.

New Girl looked scared again and reached down to get it. "That's my lucky—"

"Don't."

She froze, hand still under the bench. She looked up at me, confused again.

"Get your toy and let's go." I stood up, annoyed and sorry for her.

"It's not really a toy," she muttered.

"I don't want to know."

Showing her the ropes was going to be a lot of work.

I glanced over as she picked up the weird rabbit foot with both hands, a sad look on her face. I wanted to tell her, *You're lucky charm ain't workin'*, but then I felt bad, and remembered how awful Sheri was to me during my early days. "Did you see the beach?" I asked.

She looked up, eager and innocent. "I saw a little from the plane. That was my first plane ride... but no, I've never seen a real beach, I mean, like in person."

"Well, the world-famous Waikiki Beach is just a couple of blocks this way."

I caught her skinny arm in mine and led her across the street where the light had just turned. Scads of tourists—some good potential customers—crossed with us in both directions.

The moon was almost full and lit up the white caps of the distant waves and the lacey edges of the water where it lapped gently on the beach.

"Oh, wow," New Girl said as she took in the sight. "It doesn't look real. I mean I saw all those Elvis movies but I—" She walked onto the edge of the sand and stopped, looking all around. The tall surfboards in the huge racks.

I asked, "Do you want to dip your feet in the water?"

She looked over at the edge of the water, and saw a young couple walking on the wet sand, carrying their shoes. She pulled off her well-worn Keds and ran to the water, kicking up sand. I thought of Nana's old cat in the sandbox behind her house.

I pulled off my own shoes and caught up to New Girl just as she stood in the cool glistening flat sand at the edge of the water. She smiled so big I didn't want to ever tell her we had to get to work. She started to walk toward the zoo and aquarium, and into the water up to her ankles as the waves rolled in and back out. Much nicer than the jungle of Waikiki's dicier streets.

I followed her as she took it all in, the clear night sky, with more stars than she'd probably ever seen in New York City or wherever she came from before that. She checked out the tourists—families, honeymooning couples—and the old guys playing checkers on the tables along the sidewalk, and the breakwater made from big black lava rocks.

Something about seeing it all through her eyes made it even more beautiful and magical. I wanted this place to be my home, one way or another. There had to be a way to make that possible. If I worked really hard.

She finally stopped walking and turned to look at me, with a sadness in her eyes I could hardly stand to look at.

"I guess we need to—"

I cut her off. "Yes, but you need some rest. I'll point out the most popular areas on our way back to the hotel. Let's rinse off our feet and get a cab."

Relief flashed in her eyes, then turned to fear.

"But I haven't made any—"

"You can have some of my cash, just this one time."

We rinsed off our feet at the showers, then I hailed a cab. As we piled into the back seat, the soft-spoken driver asked, "Where you headed, ladies?"

"The Waikikian," I told him.

"Sounds good."

I folded some of my cash and gave it to New Girl. "You be careful with this."

"Thank you, I will." She put it in her pocket, on the side next to me.

"Look at that beautiful hotel," I said to her, leaning against her and pointing out the window on her side, while I slipped the cash out with my other hand.

"That IS a beautiful hotel!" She was distracted by the big rocking chairs along the front porch of the building, like something from the south.

"You gotta be more careful," I said softly, showing her the money.

She looked confused, then caught on.

"That's the Moana hotel. First one ever in Waikiki. Very nice," the cab driver said. "But the Waikikian is nice, too." He had a kind twinkle in his eyes as he looked at me in his rearview mirror.

New Girl took the cash from me again. She hesitated, then stuck it in her bra.

At the Waikikian, I paid the cab driver and gave him a nice tip, grateful he didn't ask questions about where we were from, why we were out so late, or what had brought us to the islands. As he took the cash from me, he held my hand for a moment, sandwiched between his. Warm hands. He said, "You ladies be careful."

After we got out of the car, New Girl gave me a funny look.

"What?" I asked.

"I think he *likes* you."

What was this, junior high? "Don't be silly, he just liked the nice tip I gave him."

"No, before that, did you see how he looked at you?"

Silly young girl. What did she know? Nothing. I did like how he held my hands, so warm and gentle. Maybe I'd run into him again. Someday.

Chapter Nineteen

Big Secrets

New Girl didn't know much about anything, but she was right about that driver. One of Marvin's less-new girls, Jenny, came out too and figured out before I did what a great driver and person Doug was. She re-introduced me to him and he smiled so big when he saw me. He liked me enough to drop whatever he was doing and show up to help me. Even when he wasn't on duty with the cab company. That loyalty and kindness was something I didn't yet appreciate enough—either in myself or other people.

In spite of my reservations, and how I was meeting other people who were much kinder to me, I stayed loyal to Marvin. I remember my Nana saying something about the *devil you know* which I didn't completely understand but figured it meant something like everyone has a bit of devil in them.

That first time in Hawaii, Marvin didn't stay long. "Too hot and muggy," he said, and went back to New York after just a few days. "You stay here a few more weeks if you like, Sweetheart," he told me, with that smooth as maple syrup feel to his voice, and his hand on my cheek.

I'd been thinking I wanted to stay a few more months or years, but whatever. Some of my favorite clothes and shoes hadn't fit in the one small suitcase I'd brought.

My bouncing back and forth between Hawaii and New York went on for months, and then years. The flight didn't get any shorter, for sure not any easier. Neither did dealing with Marvin.

On one especially bumpy flight back to New York, when I really didn't want to go—I'd started making friends—I kept thinking about all those honeymoon couples holding hands on the beach, sometimes in matching flower-print outfits. All my tired old knight-in-shining-armor ideas about Marvin were no longer so shiny. It got harder and harder to kid myself about what I really meant to him. I thought about how my mom's marriages and boyfriends didn't give me much of an example of what love should look like despite the variety. And, what a difference a calm husband versus an angry, scary husband could be. Even Mom's alleged Mafia husband, the meanest and scariest, she loved the most. Was I doomed to become my mother and repeat her mistakes?

By the time I got to Marvin after that very long plane ride, he got an earful from me. I was tired and cranky and didn't want to be back in New York, even in the summertime. When I questioned if he loved me or ever had, he said he would prove to me I was his favorite.

"How are you going to do that?" I demanded, surprising myself at how loud my voice was.

"We'll get married," he said. "Just you and me from now on."

I was stunned. Disbelieving. And relieved at the same time. Would he get down on one knee? None of this seemed real. I looked around the latest hotel room where he'd been staying. Not so different from so many other hotel rooms I'd seen.

"Will you marry me?" He asked when I didn't say anything.

I wasn't one of those girly-girls who always dreamed about her wedding. But I had a competitive side, from my days of playing hockey. Like to win him over the other girls? Be the favorite player on the team? At least feel special for a day?

"Ok," I finally replied.

"Don't sound *too* excited," he said. Hard to tell if he was annoyed or amused.

"I'm just... surprised. I will. I do. I mean, great!"

I called my sister Vivian to tell her I was getting married. "To Marvin?" she asked, with some fear, maybe disbelief in her voice, I couldn't tell, and wished for a second I could've told her in person.

"Of course, Marvin. Aren't you happy for me?"

"Well sure, if you're happy. Tell me all the details—when, where?"

"At his mom's house there in Buffalo. Next month. Then we're going on a honeymoon in the Poconos."

"A honeymoon, even, that's great!" She sounded more excited about the honeymoon than the wedding.

Or maybe that's how I felt? I hadn't had a whole three days off since... well never unless you counted those times in the hospital, when I almost died.

"The Poconos sounds fun, do you think you'll go white-water rafting?"

"That sounds fun. I hope so."

Vivian helped me round up our brother and sisters and even a sitter so Nana could come. Marvin's mom's house wasn't so huge that it could fit THAT many people, like all of Nana's kids, but all my favorite people were going to be there so I started getting excited.

I found a beautiful dress that fit me right off the rack, which was good since I didn't have a whole lot of time for alterations. The simple satin dress had a matching big floppy white hat that reminded me of one of Nana's old paint-by-numbers pictures, with a lady in a yellow hat. She had hung on Nana's kitchen wall so long the yellow was almost white like *my* hat.

"You look like something out of a fairy tale!" the sales lady said to me. I liked that idea. I found some white satin shoes with sequins and lace that were surprisingly comfortable for how fancy they were. I pictured myself wearing them for other things in the future, maybe walking around the house, taking care of the babies Marvin and I would adopt, since I couldn't have kids the normal way. Insides too busted up.

Marvin had me working all the way up to the day of the wedding.

"How else are we going to pay for all this stuff?" he asked, looking at the price tag on my dress that'd I'd hung so carefully on the back of a door. He drove down early. I had to fly the same day.

The nice sales lady had given me a clear bag with a zipper, so it was easy to see my wedding dress as I carried it through the airport, along with my hat box—which barely fit in the overhead compartment of the airplane. I folded the dress in half on my lap and hoped it wasn't getting too smooshed.

After they shut the airplane door, it felt like we sat there for forever, not pushing back like I expected. I kept looking at my watch as minutes passed since the scheduled departure time. My arms sweated on the plastic. The dress kept sliding in my lap, like it wanted to escape down the aisle and away.

Finally the pilot stepped out of the cockpit and picked up the phone to make an announcement.

"Sorry for the delay, folks. One of my lights came on and it's probably nothing but we just have to have a mechanic check it out to be sure. I'll give you an update as soon as I know more."

I felt the blood drain from my face. A flight attendant taking orders for free drinks did a trouble-take when she saw me. "Are you okay, darlin'? You look a little pale."

"As white as this *wedding dress*?" I asked, angry and scared at the same time. "My wedding is today. Do you have any idea how long—"

"Your wedding is TODAY!?" she echoed, looking at the dress in my lap. "And this is the dress?"

"Yes, and I—"

"Her wedding is TODAY!" she shouted toward the front of the plane, where the door to the cockpit still stood open.

The pilot was on his feet and headed our way.

"Can we hang this up for you?" asked the flight attendant.

"Yes, please, that would be great."

She passed the pilot in the narrow aisle and he knelt down right next to me—the way Marvin had *not* when proposing. "I'm so sorry for the delay, miss." he said softly, his hand taking one of my sweaty ones. "Congratulations on your big day."

"Thank you."

"If it's any consolation, this mechanical hiccup has happened to me before on this aircraft, and it's always nothing. The indicator light in the cockpit is likely what needs replacing. I'll tell them to make it snappy—we're in a hurry!"

I could listen to him talk all day using words no one I knew ever used, like *aircraft* and *indicator light*. I trusted every single thing he said, he sounded so confident. Wouldn't it be nice if life was like an airplane ride, with all the bumps along the way, but someone so confident and smart like this man making sure you get to where you're supposed to be?

I could hear Nana's voice in my head, as if answering my question, *That's what* GOD *does, sweetheart. Helps you get around the bumps and dark clouds in life.*

Was this pilot going up against God, who didn't want me to go to my own wedding? And he used the words, SNAPPY and HURRY? That didn't sound like a good idea when it came to flying. I wanted to ask about that, but he gave my shoulder a reassuring squeeze and headed back to the cockpit.

"Would you like some champagne, my dear?" The nice flight attendant who'd hung up my dress was back with a bottle and a glass.

I didn't drink very often, and I didn't feel like I had much to toast, but she was so eager for me to have one. "Sure." Maybe this would pass the time faster, and make me worry less about what the pilot was doing to *hurry* us along.

Chapter Twenty

Not-so-Big Wedding

When we finally landed in Buffalo, the pilot asked all the other passengers to remain seated while they let me get off first. "Let's make sure this beautiful bride gets to her wedding on time."

The whole plane cheered, and I felt hopeful again. If an airplane full of strangers was this happy for me, how could I not be happy for myself?

When I got off the plane, Vivian was there at the gate to meet me. "Wow, first off the plane," she said.

I dropped my bag and hat box, and hugged her hard, still holding my dress by the hanger. "They were so nice to me!"

"That's great, and I want to hear all about it, but we have to hurry." She picked up my bag and hat box and started walking fast.

There was that word *hurry* again. I said a silent prayer of thanks that the plane had made the short trip safely in spite of my fears about what kind of duct tape or chewing gum they used to get it going.

I caught up to her and she glanced at me. "Your hair looks cute." She'd agreed to help me fix my hair for the wedding, and I could hear the worry in her voice, like, *What are we going to do with that*? My hair was the shortest it had been in a long time, which was easier to take care of and also made it harder for anyone to grab, a john or Marvin.

"Don't worry," I told her, pointing to the hat box, "The hat and the veil will cover most of it."

Turns out, Vivian helping me get ready was my favorite part of the whole wedding, including the honeymoon. When the priest asked, "Any reason this couple should not be joined in holy matrimony, speak now or forever hold your peace," I swear it felt like a very long pause as if he hoped someone would speak up. Then Marvin put the ring on the wrong finger—my right hand instead of left. I wondered, is he high again or does he not really want to do this? Or both? I switched it, hoping no one would notice. I kept wondering if anyone would mention it, all through the short reception, which also felt like a hurry, especially the way Marvin rushed me out of there.

He kept reminding me, all the way to the Poconos, that it had to be kept secret back in the city. He didn't want me to tell the other girls because that might *cause problems*. He said, "It'll just be our special secret." Then the whole three days we were there, he just did more drugs and we never left the room. I cried the whole time and begged him to quit. He was killing himself.

He smacked me, harder than ever, and said, "Don't tell me what to do!"

So much for "happily ever after."

I didn't know what to do to get him to change, but I knew I couldn't control him. I didn't even understand all my confused and complicated feelings for him, like why should I even care? I saw a lawyer back in the city and got the whole bullshit marriage thing annulled. He didn't even seem to care. Nothing mattered to him. Any control I had was only over myself. So, I quit eating. Maybe it would get his attention. That's how I'd learned to get my mom's attention as a kid. Get sick. I could make myself skinny like that New Girl in Waikiki who I never saw again and never asked about. Skinny like every model I'd ever seen on TV. I figured being skinny might get me more money, if nothing else, since all the sexy images in magazines and on TV were skinny girls. Barbie, too. I got so skinny my bones stuck out. Collar bones, hip bones, ribs. Marvin paid no attention.

One fall night on the streets in New York City, streets made even colder when you're just skin and bones, a tingling spread from the top of my head to my limbs and brought me to the ground like I'd been cold cocked. All 90 pounds of me rattled like a skeleton whacking against the sidewalk.

"Fuck!" A familiar high voice shouted. I blacked out.

The voice belonged to Jenny, another one of Marvin's girls, not mean like Sheri, and Jenny got extra points in my book for introducing me to Doug.

The thought of Doug calmed me for a moment.

In the ambulance, I heard voices, then I blinked and started to see. Jenny's forehead scrunched together as she peered at me. "Maria, can you hear me?"

In my head I answered her. Not sure I said it out loud before I faded out again. I woke up in a hospital bed and she was still there, looking worried. "Why are you here?"

She smiled. "You're awake! You know you could've died."

Not the first time I almost died, or ended up in the hospital. I thought about all the times before. Too many times. The time they had to wire my jaw shut because Marvin had hit me so hard. Got more customers after that because I looked more like a kid, with braces. When those other girls stabbed me and left me for dead. What was wrong with the human race?

How many times in hospitals and doctors' offices had they told me I'd never have children? What was my life about anyway? I looked at Jenny. She wouldn't have any answers.

"Why are you here? I thought you hated me." They all hated me, and normally that was fine. I usually liked to fly solo and let them all think I was some kind of psycho bitch.

"I don't hate you." She looked away as she said this. Was she lying? "I have to act that way so the other girls don't kick my ass. I'm not tough and scrappy like you."

The guys I used to play hockey with called me things like *tough* and *scrappy*. In her voice, I heard a touch of... admiration?

"Besides, if I didn't look after you and Marvin found out he'd kill me." She chuckled like it was a joke but we both knew it wasn't. "You gotta eat something." She pointed at the nearby tray, with each dish covered in plastic wrap, even the green Jello. "Otherwise you ARE going to die. The nurse even said."

I squinted at her, doubting. "If I did die, would Marvin even notice? I mean besides the money." My voice sounded pitiful, even to me. Like it got skinny, too.

"Fuck Marvin. He doesn't give a shit about us. Why should we give a shit about him?"

He promised to love me forever, I wanted to tell her, even made it official and married me. But I'd been sworn to secrecy. Maybe he'd done the same with her? Why had I never thought of that before? Why was he so desperate for me to keep it a secret? Maybe we weren't even married, officially. He could've slipped the judge some cash while I wasn't looking to not submit the official paperwork, or maybe he messed up his name or birthday on purpose so it wouldn't be valid.

Who knew what kind of tricks he'd pulled to keep me tied to him? Had I wasted my time and money hiring that lawyer to get the annulment as soon as we got back to the city?

Anyway, this time in the hospital wasn't as bad as the times before, at least as far as how much pain I felt, physically. No broken jaw, no blown-up ovaries. I had some scrapes on my elbows and wrists, from the seizure on the sidewalk. Minor stuff on the outside. Inside, though, I felt more broken than ever. Heartbroken. Like my spirit was broken. I knew I couldn't keep going on like this. What did I have to live for? Nothing. Not a real marriage. Not a real love. Not a real life.

A nurse in bright pink scrubs and a giant pink smile came into the room and talked to me like I was a little kid. "How are we doing? Did we have something to eat, yet?"

"She doesn't want to eat," Jenny said.

Pink nurse sat on the bed next to me and pulled the tray over. She started peeling plastic wrap off while talking a mile a minute.

"You HAVE to eat, sweetheart."

I feared she might try the old *here comes the airplane* trick like I was in a high chair. I pulled the sheet up over my head and promised—lied, "Later."

Jenny half-whispered, "I have an idea."

"What's that?" the cheerful nurse asked her.

She whispered something else.

"Okay, well, I'll come back later and check on you both."

Jenny knew how to play tricks, too.

"What's your idea?" I asked through the sheet. "Or was that just to get her to leave?"

"She was kind of annoying, but no, I do have an idea. You might like this."

I doubted it, but I pulled down the sheet and looked at her.

"Were you serious," Jenny asked. "All that stuff you said in the ambulance?"

"What did I say in the ambulance? I thought I was out?"

"You were going on and on about how you could never have children, so what was the point of all this anyway, that they should just let you die and see what's next."

"I said all that in the ambulance? Did they think I was crazy? Is this the mental hospital?" I looked all around for clues on the walls. Nothing.

"No, just the regular hospital. But I have a secret to tell you. Promise you won't tell anyone?"

"Depends on what the secret is."

Chapter Twenty-One

Bigger Secret

The nice nurse kept interrupting our conversation, but it didn't bother me, I wasn't really listening anyway. I was a bit surprised by how Jenny was trying everything to get me to come out of my funk and eat something. She'd even run out and bought me the royal blue suede shoes she knew I wanted, that she'd seen me admire in my favorite shoe-store window. They made me smile, but I didn't put them on. Just looked at them there on the box next to bed. I liked those better than the flowers people normally brought to hospitals.

"Hey," Jenny said, "you remember that cute boy that keeps asking you out, trying to buy you stuff?"

"Gary? The sweet college kid I met in Buffalo at that New Year's Party?"

"Yeah, I got a hold of him and he's on his way." The thought of Gary showing up did warm my heart a little. After the whole marriage disaster, which of course I couldn't tell Jenny about. I also couldn't tell her about how I'd hired a lawyer and gotten the whole thing annulled, making me feel like my life was nothing. A huge waste. No way out. Marvin didn't even care, seemed more interested in his drugs. And now, Marvin hadn't even come to the hospital.

Mostly to be nice but also to distract myself, I asked, "What was that secret you started to tell me before the nurse came in?"

"Oh, right. Scatterbrain me. I—" she leaned over and lowered her voice to a whisper. "I'm pregnant, but I don't want it. Plan to get an abortion."

"Okay." I didn't know where she was going with this or why she thought that was such a big secret. That kind of thing wasn't so rare. Maybe she didn't want Marvin to know since that's how he kept girls tied to him forever, by being their baby-daddy. Except that *they* were the ones doing all the money earning.

"But here's the thing, I know you can't have a baby, and so, what if I skipped the abortion, and just gave you the baby? Even better than blue suede shoes, right?"

For years Marvin had been dragging me to doctors to try to get me pregnant, I'd get my hopes up about the thought of having a baby just to be disappointed, again and again, until he finally gave up and did the marriage thing to keep me tied to him.

I sat up straighter in that hospital bed. "Do you really mean it?"

"Sure, you can have this baby." She rubbed her belly.

"But, what about Marvin?"

"I have an idea for that, too."

I picked up the green Jell-o and pulled off the plastic wrap. Suddenly, just at the thought of being fake-pregnant, I felt hungry. "I'm listening, talk."

Before Jenny had a chance to spell out her whole idea, Gary showed up, looking so worried it almost broke my heart. "Are you okay, sweetness?" He asked, out of breath at my bedside. The fact that he rushed to my side, when Marvin hadn't, and seemed so concerned about my well-being, made me think I shouldn't have assumed he wasn't really interested in me for me, but more for all the cash I could make. My self-esteem messing with my ability to have a normal relationship.

Ideas about having a baby made me more hopeful and less cynical.

"I'm okay," I said. He glanced at Jenny. "This is... my friend Jenny." It felt weird to call her that. How long had it been since I considered someone a friend?

"Nice to meet you. You're the one who... got her here?"

She smiled and nodded.

"Thank you so much." Before he had a chance to walk around the bed to shake her hand or hug her, we heard yelling in the hall. Marvin.

"I don't give a fuck how many people are allowed—"

He filled the whole doorway, with a nurse trailing behind. He stopped short when he spotted Gary, who stood up as tall as he could, and faced Marvin—the tension thick in the air. They might've been brothers, or at least cousins, they looked so alike. I guess I had a type. But Gary was the small, gentler, college-boy version of the much tougher and more frightening Marvin. The nurse behind him scurried away.

Marvin took a deep breath. "Who the fuck are you?"

"Please don't," I begged. Not wanting to see Gary get clobbered.

Marvin glanced at me and opened his mouth to say something, when Gary went OFF, poking Marvin in the chest.

"That poor girl needs rest, not yelling." Marvin's eyes went wide, so did Jenny's. Gary continued, "Who the fuck are YOU to come in here shouting and not even asking how she is?" He poked Marvin in the chest again. "You need to get lost and don't even THINK about coming back here until you calm the FUCK down, and act like a gentleman."

Marvin nearly lost his balance, stepping back away from Gary. Rapid footsteps in the hallway caused him to glance over his shoulder. Security that the nurse had called? I never knew. I looked at Gary with a whole new level of respect and affection. Thinking... he'd make an excellent dad.

He sat down next to me after Marvin disappeared. Looked relieved, exhausted, and mad.

"Wow, Gary," Jenny said, "people don't normally stand up to Marvin like that."

"He had no right," he said, more gently, turning to me. "You okay?"

"More than okay," I replied, grinning so hard my cheeks hurt. "Hey while you're here, listen to this crazy idea Jenny was just telling me..."

Chapter Twenty-Two

Immaculate Deception

Gary's bravery, standing up to Marvin, inspired me to be more brave. He was only 21 years old, and I was a 24, going on much older having been through so much and nearly killed several times. If that college kid could be brave, so could I.

Together, Gary, Jenny and I hatched a plan—a weird, beautiful, bold and brave plan—and by some miracle we kept it going for the many months leading up to the big day. Including the various sized pillows I stuffed under my shirt to fake my own pregnancy—while watching Jenny's belly expand with a real, kicking, growing baby.

By this time in my life, I had told loads of lies and tricked many, many people. So lying to good, honest, well-meaning folks, like those at the hospital and Gary's mom, came a little too easy. I was starting to believe my own bullshit, wondering what else I might get away with just by acting confident. Acting like I knew what I was doing.

This would be the biggest trick I ever pulled, beyond those on johns or cops, or would-be attackers. I didn't even think about the victims of my huge fraud. I was too excited and happy to think about right or wrong, victims or crimes, lies or truths. All I could think of was the prize.

Finally the day came and Jenny announced, "It's time!" Her water had broken and her contractions were contracting. So excited, we grabbed the bag for the hospital and hobbled out to the parking lot.

The car was gone. Stolen. Very bad timing. Someone pulled a not-so-nice trick on us.

"Shit!" Jenny shouted. "Can you believe this?" She started to laugh or cry. I wasn't sure which. "We did park it here, right?"

"We did. I'll call a cab." I helped Jenny back inside, and started dialing.

"Yellow cab," a gruff voice answered.

"How fast can you get to..." I rattled off our address and held my breath.

"Let's see," the guy said so slowly. At least it seemed slow to me.

"We got a pregnant lady here, can you make it snappy?"

He promised just a few minutes, and we weren't very far from the hospital.

As the minutes ticked by, Jenny had more contractions. I worried aloud, "Maybe I should have called an ambulance?"

"Nah, that's too much money," Jenny reassured me. "I think we still got some time. And babies are expensive, you gotta keep every dime you can."

I let out a breath and hoped she was right about the timing.

The cab driver nearly caught air going through one intersection. I worried all the bouncing wasn't good for the baby. I figured the driver really didn't want his cab messed up. I kept asking if she felt okay. Kept saying silent prayers.

"Can you believe that shit?" Jenny said as the hospital came into sight. "Go to have the baby and the damn car is GONE." She shook her head and started giggling and I did too. Nerves, excitement and worry.

I practically threw the cash at the driver as we got out of the cab and hurried inside the huge building, bustling with doctors, nurses, medical staff, and other patients. I couldn't wait until the moment when I walked out with a *baby*. Me, a mom! I would love that little girl so much, pouring into her all the love I'd never had as a child.

In the halls of the hospital, happy I didn't have to wear the pillows anymore, I held my shoulders back, faking confidence. Fake it till you make it, I'd heard somewhere and told myself often. As we made our way to the maternity ward, we paused a couple of times for more contractions. Jenny waddled awkwardly. I could barely stop myself from skipping and breaking into song. I patted her shoulders, and her soft brown hair when she'd bend over in pain. "Breathe. We're almost there, you're doing great."

I kept hearing a song in my head, "We Are Family" by Sister Sledge, "I got all my sisters and me!" Jenny was the closest thing I'd had to a sister besides my long-lost little sisters and Vivian, who still thought I was nuts for having anything to do with Marvin, never mind having his baby. And the last few months, especially, I felt like a big sister, taking care of Jenny, keeping her away from Marvin, his drugs, his temper. Mostly his temper. Our pimp had no interest in the baby growing in Jenny. His baby. I had hoped he might ease off some on the pot smoking when I'd shown him the sonogram. Instead he'd just grunted. When I told him, "It's a girl!" His reply was: "Shit. Just what we need," and he left, gone for days. His disappearances kept getting longer and longer. Didn't seem like just a pot problem anymore.

The waiting area of the maternity ward wasn't too crowded. A nice lady at the desk gave us a clipboard with a form to fill out. The walls had cute wallpaper covered with different safari animals. The lions looked like some cartoon version of mean. That's how I needed to think of Marvin. Over there. Something I could stare down and deal with. Let him believe he's king of the jungle. Roar sometimes. Swagger. Hold his head high.

"Look at those cute giraffes," I said to Jenny, attempting to distract her from the latest round of contractions.

"Tall, like this baby's going to be. *Your* baby." She gave me a weak smile, putting on a brave face. I smiled back and continued filling out the form, with all *my* information. Just like we'd planned, since that day she called me and said, "Last chance. I'm doing it today, unless you want it." By *doing it* she meant having an abortion. She didn't want to say the words.

I hesitated on the part of the form where they wanted to know about the father. I could put Marvin's name in there. But, like he said: "This is your deal. Leave me out of it. I don't want no baby."

Could've put Gary's name on there. My college-boy boyfriend had been so sweet about the whole fake pregnancy thing. Even telling his mother the child was his, or at least letting her assume that. He was a terrible liar. Best for him to just let people jump to the conclusion.

At the end of the line for *father's name*, a box labeled N/A jumped out at me. Yes. Not Applicable. Not available. Not around. Not anyone else's. This was *my* baby. I hoped checking that box would also avoid questions from the hospital staff about where the father was during the delivery. The plan was to let my family show up later. After the deal was done. After the baby was here. *My* baby.

Jenny squeezed my hand with her latest contraction. After all this pain and trouble, what if she changed her mind? Sometimes that happened. But how often? You'd hear about people doing *legal* adoptions where the birth mother saw the baby and changed her mind. I had no paperwork, no legal anything. Just a promise made by a friend who still clung to some of her Catholic roots. I did trust her, though.

We'd grown very close during those months. Me holding back her hair while she threw up. I'd even told her, part way into that third trimester, about how Marvin and I had been married. She listened and didn't seem too surprised. Joked he'd be a crappy father anyway, and it was smart of me to end the marriage sooner rather than later.

Each time Jenny squeezed my hand while we waited for her to be dilated enough, I thanked God mine was only the pain in my hand. Her face scrunched in agony. Sweat dripped from the hair stuck to the sides of her face. Occasionally a nurse would come by and check on her.

I'd seen babies born in movies and on TV, and of course I knew that wasn't real or anywhere near that simple. Still. The minutes seemed like hours. Once I almost said *All this waiting is like torture,* but then I looked at the pain in Jenny's face and bit my tongue. Could anyone ever give a greater gift than a baby? Their own flesh and blood. I brought more ice chips and tried to quiet my own growling stomach. No way would I eat something when she couldn't.

We spent forever, hours and hours, listening to a range of feelings shouted ("I hate you, this all your fault"), grunts, and cries for help from nearby rooms and outside in the hall. I worried if our long wait was normal. Would the baby get squashed if she stayed in there too long? Would Gary and his mother show up too soon, unable to wait any longer? Catch the two of us—me suddenly not pregnant, and some stranger not yet dilated enough?

Finally, finally, after what felt like days, they rolled Jenny out, heading for the delivery room.

"Almost there, Jenny! I mean, Mary!" I said, catching myself on our name switch.

One of the nurses looked at me funny.

"I'm just so excited I'm getting all confused."

No one noticed my lame explanation about the names. Jenny shrieked in pain.

For just a second, I wondered if her shriek was real or if she was just covering for me. Her acting and lying skills had taught me a lot about surviving in our business. The next shriek pierced my eardrums. No way fake.

"Give me some fuckin' drugs!"

I knew she was really in pain. We'd talked about the drugs. She didn't like the idea at all. We'd seen what drugs did to Marvin. Didn't want to end up like him.

"In a minute, sweetheart," a kind nurse steered the bed into the delivery room.

"Uh oh," I heard. "Breech?"

I asked, "Is this normal?"

"You have to wait outside," the nurse pointed toward the door. I stole a glance at Jenny. She looked like she was in horror movie. Not a TV baby birth.

"Out of the room, please," the nurse said."

Another nurse shouted, "Her pressure's dropping."

The heavy door slammed shut behind me. The walls spun.

No. No. "This can't be happening." I said to no one.

I heard Jenny scream one last time. Then silence. Deathly quiet.

No, please God, no. I leaned against the wall next to the door, sweat rolling down my face. My stomach growled loudly, terrible timing.

A nurse ran out, looked at me and said, "It's going to be a while. Go have a seat." She tilted her head toward the waiting room. I started for that door, but noticed a sign in the hall that said Chapel and headed that way instead.

The tiny room with just a couple of pews felt impossibly quiet after the choir of laboring pregnant ladies. A dark-haired woman sat in the first pew. She turned toward me, got up, drying tears from her eyes, and nodded as she left me alone. Tiny dust particles danced in the sunlight coming in through a high stained-glass window. I knelt in front of the huge cross. Avoiding the stare of Jesus.

What if my decision to keep her baby instead of her ending the pregnancy meant they BOTH died? Did that break the thou shall not kill rule? I was trying to SAVE a life. We had a plan. The plan had been working.

"Please let them both be okay," I said in a whisper. How long since the last time I'd tried to pray? Like for real, pray. Not just some wish about not getting killed. I prayed for that all the time. A couple times even praying that I WOULD get killed. But I didn't really mean it. Usually.

I pressed my hands together, my elbows on the wooden rail. My eyes shut hard.

"Lord, please, if you can hear me, if you consider me your child after all of my sins, please let this baby live, and Jenny. I'll be the best mother that could ever be. I will love her so much. Give her everything she could ever need. Please just let her be okay. Let them be okay.

"I'm going to name her Kristian." My own words startled me a little. "And I will raise her as a good Christian. Just please Lord... Just..."

I begged and promised for a while. Hoping so hard.

The whoosh of the door opening brought me back to reality. I stood up, crossed myself, kissed my tiny cross, and turned around to leave. The distraught man at the threshold avoided my eyes, while holding the door open for me.

On the way back I found a vending machine and scarfed down a candy bar, feeling guilty about eating but not wanting to pass out from hunger. I wandered the long empty hall outside the room where I'd left Jenny. I could hear nothing. Just murmuring that might've been in my head. I remembered the nurse's orders and went back to the waiting room. Stared down some cartoon lions on the wall. Looked at the smiling, playful giraffes.

Delilah.

Was it bad luck to have a name before the baby came? Had I jinxed it somehow?

After forever, when the wallpaper animals started spinning and dropping dead in my imagination, a woman came in and looked around the waiting room, then she asked, "Are you Jenny?"

"No—" I caught myself, remembering our name swap, and I shook my head, "I mean yes. Is Mary okay?"

"She hemorrhaged and needed some stitches, but she's okay," she said, and smiled.

"And the baby?"

"Come see for yourself!"

I wanted to shove her out of the way and run. "Thank you, Lord," I muttered instead, pressing my gold cross into my chest.

A bundled baby flew by in a blur, carried by another nurse. They'd cleaned, wrapped, and whisked her away, to what I assumed was the nursery, like you see on TV, babies lined up row by row in little clear boxes. I wanted to follow that nurse but knew I should check on Jenny. I poked my head into the room. Smelled like sweat.

Jenny's dark hair was sticking to the sides of her face. She looked exhausted.

She smiled weakly. "I did it."

I rushed to her side and held her hand, smoothing some of her damp hair off her forehead. "Yes you did! I'm so proud of you!"

"Did you see her?" she asked, looking around like she wasn't sure if the baby was still in the room.

"Barely. I wanted to make sure you're okay."

"I'm okay." She let her head fall back on the pillow and closed her eyes. "I couldn't have done it without you."

"But they didn't even let me in the room." I started to protest, not sure if she was being sarcastic. She did that sometimes.

She opened her eyes and looked at me hard. "I mean the whole thing. You took better care of me than anyone. Ever. You're gonna be a great momma. Now go find your baby."

My eyes filled with tears. A little part of me, okay a huge part of me, worried that when she actually had the baby and held it in her arms, she wouldn't want to let go. She'd change her mind. And what could I do? Nothing. Another huge part of me worried that I'd be no good as a mom. What did I know about motherhood? My own mother killed herself—and didn't even do that well—took her a bunch of tries to finally get it done. But Jenny was right. I took excellent care of her pregnant, uncomfortable, complicated self. Even working long hours to keep Marvin off our backs. I could do this.

First we had to finish our con job here at the hospital. Although it wasn't really a con because that's like a crime where someone is getting ripped off. I thought of it like a performance, almost like those plays on Broadway I loved to go to when I had a chance. But here the people we put on the show for were the hospital people. For the next performance, we had my people who'd so far believed the whole fake pregnancy with the bigger and bigger pillows under my clothes. I needed to call them, especially my boyfriend and his mother—who just couldn't wait to be a grandmother. I felt bad tricking her like this but the truth would be too much for that nice square lady to handle. And I didn't want to risk the hospital people figuring out what was going on if she somehow slipped and let it out.

"Excuse me," I asked the one remaining nurse cleaning up the delivery room, "are you moving her to another room?"

"Yes, they'll be right in to take you to the recovery room, and you can hold the baby!"

The nurse smiled at Jenny, whose face turned serious. Not what the nurse probably expected. She cleared her throat nervously and left the room.

"I don't want to hold it," Jenny whispered to me.

I was relieved she hadn't already. "That's okay, you don't have to," I patted her hands that clenched the sheets. "Maybe better if you don't." Didn't most of those stories of women changing their mind happen when the birth mom held the baby and... Better if you don't, I repeated in my head.

The next person who came in cleaned up Jenny some before they rolled her down the hall to a room. I wondered if they wanted to make sure the new moms looked a little more presentable before they were out and about where other moms-to-be might see them. "How do you feel?" she asked.

"Kinda ripped apart," Jenny said. Did she mean *physically* or did her heart feel torn, too?

The nurse had a quick peek under the sheet and said, "Looks like the bleeding stopped." Jenny and I both grimaced. "So you should be up and on your feet soon."

Like in about 10 minutes? I wanted to ask, since she had to pretend to be the friend very soon, while I took her place in bed. Jenny and I exchanged a nervous glance.

After they wheeled her into the recovery room, and she was resting comfortably, I went to find a payphone.

"Hello?" Breathless, Gary answered on the first ring.

"Gary, it's me." I spoke fast, like someone might catch me at any minute. Or I might miss when they brought Kristian into that room. "She's here. I gotta get back there, it's room 409."

"That's great! Did they give you a weight and le—"

"Gotta go, I don't want to miss her." I almost hung up the phone but could still hear his voice.

"Wait, wait, what do you mean 'miss her'?"

"I haven't actually met her yet, they're going to bring her in any second." Saying the words made my heart beat even faster.

"Okay, well, we're on our way. I love—"

I'd hung up before he could finish. I hadn't said these words back to him yet, ever. I ran back to the room, pushing that thought out of my head.

Jenny sat on the guest chair, in her regular clothes.

"What are you—"

"You'd better change, they'll be back any second." She pointed to the hospital gown on the empty bed.

I pulled off my clothes, setting a new world record for speed. I shoved them in the drawer next to the bed, and looked at Jenny.

"That was fast."

"Are you okay? Does it hurt?"

"Don't worry about me, Momma. You look too perfect. She leaned over and messed up my hair, dipped her hand in the cup of water on the nightstand and wetted my bangs, just as a nurse came in. Luckily not one we'd seen before. We looked a bit alike anyway. Dark hair, similar size.

"Look who's here," she said, turning around so we could see the bundle in her arms.

"Oh!" I gasped and reached out, faking a wince, doing my best acting job.

"Are you okay?" The nice nurse asked, not even looking at Jenny.

"I'm great," I waved her over, thinking hurry up, why so slow? Let me see her!

She placed the bundle in my arms, and time stopped. The nugget squirmed and opened her eyes, looked right at me. The rest of the world fell away. She blinked twice and closed her eyes again. I was in love. Those tiny lips. All that dark hair. Her tiny, perfect fingers. Cute little nose. The most beautiful creature to ever live.

"Do we have a name yet?" the nice nurse asked.

"Yes, this is Kristian." I kissed her on her pink forehead. "I love you more than you could ever know. "

I breathed in her new baby smell. My cheeks felt funny from smiling so hard. Time slipped by.

Jenny's face was hard to read, which was weird, because the main thing I'd learned since getting into the business was how to read a face. She smiled but it looked strained. Because of the pain her body still felt? Because she didn't want to give up this baby? I didn't want to ask. I just smiled and said, "She's perfect. Thank you so much." Part of me wanted to ask, "Do you want to hold her?" because holding her was so wonderful. We'd discussed this before though. Jenny wasn't even looking at her. She looked at me or around the room, never at the baby.

When Gary and his mom showed up in record time, I didn't have to ask the new grandma. She reached out her arms as she walked in the room.

"Is that my grandbaby?" She beamed so hard I thought the lines on her face might get stuck in that huge smile.

She scooped her up from me as Gary came to my side and asked, "How are you doing?" He looked at me, then at Jenny.

"We're doing okay," I answered. We knew that he knew I meant Jenny, not me and the baby. Keeping this huge secret from the beaming grandma was the worst part of all this. Gary could hardly get his head around the whole thing, never mind how I earned the money to pay for everything. He loved the idea of me earning so much money, but not the idea of sharing me with others. Talked about how he'd help get me out of the life.

The unanswered question hung in the air: "Is that my grandbaby?" We just let her assume. She made goofy noises and bounced little Delilah.

"Oh, I brought my camera," she said, finally, handing the baby to Gary, whose eyes got real wide. He held onto little Delilah like she was made of glass. "That's it, Honey, you're doing fine! You're going to be a great father." She dug the camera out of her purse and looked through it, motioning for Gary to move in a little closer.

Jenny said, "I could take one of the three of you."

Gary's mom looked startled, like she'd not noticed Jenny sitting there until just then. "That would be lovely! Now who are you?"

Jenny and I exchanged glances, as Gary said, "That's Mary's good friend, Jenny."

"Nice to meet you, Jenny."

Jenny flinched when she got up to take the picture.

"Are you okay?" the grandmother asked.

"I'm fine, ma'am. Do I just press this button here?" She smiled, almost looking sincere. We'd both been in the business long enough to know just what to say and which buttons to press when.

The image of Gary cradling Delilah in his arms, gave me hope for a normal life.

Sadly, my relationship with him eventually fizzled like all my romantic relationships. We were too young and inexperienced to handle all we faced.

I had so many lessons to learn about all the different kinds of love. And how to take care of a tiny human. I also had some very strong opinions about the best way to love this little girl, and that's exactly what I planned to do.

Chapter Twenty-Three

Raising Delilah

Marvin didn't care if I went to Hawaii often, as long as I kept sending his money via Western Union. He hated to fly—was too tall for the seats, even in first class, and barely fit in the lavatories. "I can't stand being in that fuckin' can for so many hours," he complained. He didn't like not being in control, with someone else flying the plane and calling the shots.

The flight was long for little Delilah—even when she slept most of the way. The flight attendants were always nice, and sometimes walked her up and down the aisle to give me a break.

Hawaii was so much more laid back and warm than New York. I didn't have to worry about keeping my baby from freezing her tiny toes off. I loved to watch her play outside, growing up so fast, crawling then walking faster than most kids her same age. Finally, I bought a one-way ticket, rented an apartment, and enrolled Delilah in the best preschool I could find.

She especially liked to sing and do crafts. The bigger the mess the better. One activity—about birds—had both crafts and a song. In New York, we had so many pigeons, or as my sister Vivian called them, "Rats with wings." In Hawaii, we had lots of different kinds of birds. At the many outdoor restaurants, tourists would feed the too-many doves and pigeons. But we also had mynah birds, not quite as black as crows, and when my growing-up-too-fast little Delilah would spot one, she'd sing the song she learned about them in preschool.

"Sassy little mynah bird, with your funny walk, my you are a noisy bird, all you do is talk talk talk!" As a toddler, she'd say *mynah* more like *my-ma*.

Once she brought me a construction-paper mynah bird she made in school. I scooped her onto my lap and thanked her for the gift.

"Thank you sweetheart, I love it!" I was running out of room on the refrigerator to put her latest art, but I'd find a spot.

"I love you," she said. Her *love* sounded like *wuv* and it was the sweetest sound I ever heard. Sweetness I never heard from Marvin. All the late nights and mean customers and Marvin's violence were worth it for moments like this. She kissed me and touched my face with her sticky three-year-old fingers.

"Did you use paste?" I asked, hoping she hadn't eaten any of it.

"Yup."

"Can I help you with your fingers?"

She nodded as I pulled some handy-wipes out of my purse. Mostly I used them to tidy up the johns, something I didn't want to think about while cleaning my daughter's beautiful fingers.

Soon after that, Halloween crept up on us and she asked if she could dress as a mynah bird, then at the last minute decided to be a princess. I liked that idea better since in my mind, she would always be my princess.

"Are you sure?" I asked. "Because you are kinda like a mynah bird."

"With my funny walk?" She waddled with her arms out, more like a penguin.

I laughed. "No, cuz' all you do is TALK TALK TALK!" I teased and she giggled. I loved the sound of her laugh so much.

At Christmastime, she learned the twelve days of Christmas, Hawaiian style, complete with five big fat pigs (like you'd have at a luau, buried in the ground) instead of five gold rings. Rather than a partridge in a pear tree, it was, "...and one mynah bird in one papaya tree." She'd laugh and laugh, especially when she got all the way to the *twelve televisions*.

I'd make sure, with each passing year, she'd learn how to speak both that broken-English pidgin and good English. "One mynah bird in one papaya tree," was fine when singing with her friends, but I also wanted her to get a good job someday and she'd need to speak well for that. Better than me.

I hired the best childcare and tutors money could buy.

As Kris grew and got more complicated, so did my list of support staff, and methods of doing business. I called that nice cab driver all the time. Doug was Delilah's favorite ride to and from school on rainy days or when I didn't have time to walk her to her elementary school. Half the time he wouldn't take my money, insisting, "*I'm* not doing *you* a favor, *you're* doing *me* one. That little girl always makes me smile." I'd have to hide cash in his glove compartment when he wasn't looking. Usually I spent my time with men *taking* the money, not *stashing* it for them to find later.

With all the bills for tutors and educational toys and supporting both Jenny and Marvin, I also got more creative at helping myself to bigger tips. I was quick to abort those missions if anything was the slightest bit off—always being super careful cuz' now I REALLY couldn't end up in jail. My skills got to the point where I could pick the pockets of pants left casually on the floor using my toes.

I confessed this to Vivian once when she came to visit us. She laughed and said, "You always were like a little monkey, even on the monkey bars back in elementary school." By this time in my life, she had given up on trying to convince me to choose another career. When I asked her about it, she told me, "I'm just glad to see you far away from that good-for-nothing Marvin. And I'm happy to see you're happy as a mom."

I'd also told her about the annulment, and how the baby wasn't really mine. She took it all in stride. Just wanted me to be happy and for my baby to be safe and happy, too.

I did NOT tell her how I was still sending money to both Marvin and Jenny. They both knew they could yank my strings any time they wanted—all they had to do was threaten to take away my baby. Even though all the paperwork from the hospital and the state of New York said that Kris was my kid, and ONLY my kid, who knew what the lawyers could do to me? Or the cops or the government?

That very first lawyer of Marvin's, who didn't keep me out of Rikers, never even asked to hear my side of the story about how the money got stolen, or whether I was even who I said I was. Who knew what Marvin or Jenny might try. Not that either of them wanted to raise Kris—that's the last thing either of them wanted—but they'd sure drop hints that they might take her if I ever sent the money even the slightest bit late.

As Kris got more curious and observant, she asked harder questions. Once, I called Doug to give us a ride from Kris's elementary school directly to the Western Union. On our way there, when she figured out we weren't going directly home, she asked, "Are we going to the store painted like a mynah bird?"

"What, sweetheart? Painted?" I looked her over. She didn't get paint on her as much as she used to in preschool, but you never knew.

"The store, how the store is painted black and yellow. Like a mynah bird."

"Huh. Yeah, I guess it is. You are so smart! How did you get to be so smart?" I asked.

She shrugged her adorable shoulders. "Just born that way, I guess."

Doug chuckled from the front seat and shook his head. "She's going to be a handful, I'm telling you."

"She's already a handful, and not even five yet."

"Almost!" she shouted. "But why do we always have to go to that store? Especially since, what do you get for your money? Nothing."

She had a point. What did I get? I wanted to say, *I get to keep you, kid*, or *peace of mind*. But she was too little to understand. And I didn't want her to know. "Never mind, sweetie."

"But Mommy—"

"Let's talk about you turning five." Just then I spotted the line at the Western Union. Out the door. "Crap."

"Isn't that a bad word? And why is it crap that I'm turning five? I heard that's a GOOD age."

"Yes, that's exciting. I can't wait," I replied. "I saw that line." I pointed. "Do you mind, Doug?"

"No problem," he said, knowing the drill by now. He'd drive Kris around while I waited in line. Maybe get her some shave ice. Find out what she wanted for her birthday.

When she was small enough to carry in my arms or on my hip, I'd bring her in with me. Everyone would fawn over her and tell us how cute she was. But these days I could barely lift her up, never mind carry her on my hip for that long. Besides, some of the characters you'd see in the Western Union were pretty sketchy-looking folks.

I got out of the cab and hustled across the sidewalk. The only person outside the door was just squeezing into the tiny Western Union Office. I got a whiff of body odor and opted to wait outside until at least a couple more people left. Luckily the line moved pretty quickly. Once I was inside, all three men waiting looked me up and down, their eyes focused on my extra-large bazoombas.

The Honolulu plastic surgeons loved me, as I bought bigger and bigger boobs, hoping for bigger tips and higher-paying customers. Each surgery made me hopeful I'd hate my body less. And I would, but only for a little while.

Two of the men inside the Western Union looked extra sketchy, with ratty clothes and unwashed hair, waiting for money from parents or loved ones better off than them. Or maybe the folks on the other end wanted nothing to do with them and sent money to keep them away.

I pressed my purse against me, glad I'd not brought Delilah, and grateful the large amount of cash I had would soon be behind the glass, so no one would be tempted to try to take it from me. I hoped Doug would show up soon.

Thankfully, the woman at the counter was one of the faster workers. She could *talk story*, as they called it here, chatting while handing out cash and doing paperwork.

"Where's that adorable girl of yours?" she asked as she counted the bills I handed over.

"Hanging out with her Uncle Doug this afternoon. Planning her fifth birthday."

"Five so soon? They grow up so fast." She handed me my receipt with a big smile. "Mahalo. Have a good day."

Doug pulled up just as I stepped outside. He and Delilah were giggling about something when I slid in the back behind them.

"Hey, Mom?"

"Yes, sweetheart." I folded the receipt and stuck it in my purse.

"How come you always have to go to that place, for reals? I want to know. It smells funny in there."

I saw Doug glance at me in the rear-view mirror, like he was curious how I was going to handle this. Or maybe he was curious about the answer, himself.

"Well, sweetheart, your momma has bills to pay, and your father—" I cut myself off, before I slipped up too much.

"I thought I didn't have a father?" she asked.

Crap. Double crap. Why did she have to pay such close attention.

"You don't, really. May as well not. He's good for nothing and very far away." I hoped that explanation would satisfy her, at least until she was a bit older.

"But Mom..."

I held my breath.

"...another kid at school has a far-away dad at that dad is always sending him stuff. How come?"

"Cuz that kid has a good dad. Your dad is not so good. That's why I got us far away from him." In the rearview mirror, Doug's brow furrowed. I wondered if he'd ask more about Delilah's father. Next to him, Delilah was silent, taking in all this new information.

"I know what you should do!" she said, sitting up straight and turning around to look at me with a big smile.

"What's that, sweetness?"

"You and Doug should get married, he'd be an excellent dad."

Doug chuckled, and I saw his eyes light up. He looked at me with that sweet twinkle in his eyes I remembered from the first night I met him. He didn't say anything.

"I bet he would be, sweetie, I bet he would. Now tell me what you decided you want for your birthday," I asked, then worried for a second she'd say, *how about a new dad*.

Luckily she said, "Well Doug and I figured it out. I made a list."

She pulled the list up to show me.

"Wow, I wish you were that eager to do your homework every night."

I caught Doug's stare in the mirror each time we stopped at a light. What went through that head of his? He didn't say too much, but I could tell there was a lot going on behind those sparkling big browns, and I wasn't sure I wanted to know.

I suspected he had way more wisdom than most, and knew better what was best for me, better than I knew for myself. But I didn't ask, and he didn't say.

Chapter Twenty-Four

Who's your Daddy?

Instead of marrying Doug like Delilah suggested back when she was in kindergarten, and a few times after that, I fell for and married a tall, handsome basketball coach who reminded me a lot of all I'd hoped Marvin was going to be to me. I used to tell people Marvin was a basketball coach. And Brandon, the actual basketball coach—for a well-respected private high school in Honolulu—was also a drug rehab counselor. He seemed almost too good to be true. I didn't realize that many drug counselors are former drug users themselves. And sometimes old habits come back. Especially when the so-called recovered addict has a girl who can make loads of money, fast.

For a while, Delilah, blazing her way through elementary school, finally had her very own step dad and her very own coach and cheerleader, like I'd never had. I'd planned to quit the business forever and have a normal life. Then I started to notice what I could not ignore: Brandon's glassy eyes, his lame excuses about where he'd been and what happened to his money. Worse, his irrational behavior. Not the loving step father or husband.

On his way out of my life, he took the $5,000 cash I had in the apartment, all of my stuff including personal photos and letters I could never replace. He ran a red light fleeing the scene as I pulled up. I watched him drive away, holding back tears.

As Delilah transitioned into junior high, she didn't laugh or sing or say much at all like the little mynah bird she used to be. She did still have the sassy, and she did TALK TALK TALK, but sometimes it was TALK TALK *TALK BACK*.

One day she asked, "Can I go ice skating? Doug said he'd take us."

"Who's US?" I was sad she now found fun more outside our home than inside. At the same time, I was glad she had friends.

"Stacy from school."

"What time will you be home?" I asked.

"Before YOU'RE home from work," she said, with some attitude.

"That's not a *time*. You'll come straight home?"

When she was a toddler and slept so much as she grew, I didn't struggle to fit in my work as an *entertainer* in Waikiki. As a pre-teen, she started to notice and complain more when I wasn't there—just before she started to like it *better* when I wasn't.

"Yes, Mom, I'll come straight home."

"Do you have any homework?"

"Just a little. We'll do it there, while they Zamboni the ice."

She loved to go ice skating, *just like your mom*, I'd say to her, telling her about how I used to play hockey back in New York. Sometimes it seemed silly for her to be using her allowance to go to Ice Palace, the ridiculously cold indoor skating rink near the Aloha Stadium. Especially silly when there was beautiful weather all year round and Castle Park with water slides in the same neighborhood. Never mind all the gorgeous beaches and hiking trails. Ice Palace did seem safer, more supervised. She wasn't going to drown or get badly sunburned like I had, so long ago, when I fell asleep on the beach. Ice Palace had a snack bar, and tables and benches where she could do her homework—but would more likely be talking to high school boys. I tried not to think about that, and all the other possible dangers, as I sat home alone.

Then I got the phone call I guess I always knew it was coming. It was Jenny. Not giggling this time. Or making demands. "It's Marvin. He's gone." Her tone sounded neutral. Like she didn't care that much. Or had already moved on.

"Gone where?" I asked, but I knew. "You mean..."

"Dead. O.D.'d."

"What? Are you sure? What happened?" My brain tried to catch up.

"He'd been using more and more cocaine, and the doctor said if he kept it up he wouldn't live long. Already had one heart attack."

Heart attack. Wow. Marvin had always appeared invincible. His increasing drug use was something everyone knew about but no one dared say anything. Except his doctor, apparently.

"You know how he didn't like anyone telling him what to do."

I nodded. "That's Marvin alright."

"So he went ahead and did it anyway."

I wanted to say, *even though he knew that was suicide*. When was the last time I'd seen him happy?

We didn't talk much longer. Weren't too close anymore.

Marvin, gone forever. I let out a long breath. Felt like I'd been holding that in for years. Marvin would never try to take my baby from me. Never threaten me, or her. No more money for him at the Western Union.

"I'm sorry he's gone," I said, surprising myself some. But I was sorry, and sad. I still loved him, in a weird way. He'd been part of my life for so long. I couldn't believe he was really gone.

"Weird, huh?" She said.

"I have to go. Let me know about the funeral. My condolences." I might have said, "I'm sorry for your loss" or whatever else people said.

I hung up the phone, still stunned. Had myself a good cry. I cried for what Marvin could have been. I cried for my young self and how he ruined my life in so many ways. I cried for the father that Delilah lost, but didn't even know she had. I cried so hard I almost couldn't breathe. Not the hiccups. Remembered a time I had hiccups with Marvin in a bodega in New York in the early days. He tried to scare me to get rid of the hiccups but he just made me laugh. Then I cried for all the fun times we'd had that he would never, ever have again.

Chapter Twenty-Five

Who's your Mama?

When Delilah's real dad died, she took it in stride and didn't say much when I told her what was going on. Not long after, someone who had no right spoke to her about her family. A cab driver who wasn't Doug. I had to piece together what happened afterwards because she came home so upset she could hardly breathe, never mind talk.

She went straight to her room and slammed the door. This happened more and more lately.

"Delilah, what's wrong?" I pounded on the door when she ignored me. "What happened? Are you okay?"

She ignored me for hours. But I was more stubborn than her. Didn't leave. I knew eventually she'd have to pee. When she did, she jumped, took a deep breath, and walked past me. I waited.

When she came out, I looked her right in the eyes. "What's the matter, sweetheart?"

She looked away, then flopped on the sofa, avoiding my gaze.

"I got a ride today, from a cab driver—who wasn't Doug."

I sat down next to her. Dread hung over me.

"He knew you. He said stuff about you."

I wanted to ask what he said, but I knew.

"He called you—rude names. Said you made tons of money, he said... who knew who my father might be?"

"We've talked about your father. He's not important." I tried to keep my voice calm.

"But I don't know what you really do for a living. And who knows what other lies you might have told me? Have you lied to me about anything else?"

I looked away, thinking about all those threats her bio mom had been making when I wouldn't give her my Social Security number for who knows what kind of scam she was up to these days, all the way in Tennessee with her new husband. She'd been threatening to spill the beans and take "her daughter" back.

"There is more that you don't know, and I need to tell you. I guess you're old enough now."

When I got to the part about how I wasn't her actual blood mom, she finally reacted. "WHAT THE FUCK?"

Normally I would have yelled back, "Watch your language!" Not today. I just listened, while she used every swear word she knew. Stamped and ranted and swung her arms around. But she didn't leave. She wanted to hear my side of the story. She finally sat back down on the sofa and looked right at me, her eyes red and damp.

"I wanted to tell you everything, sweetheart. But you were too young. You know you'll always be my little girl."

She just stared. "When were you planning to tell me?" she shouted.

Never. Damn cab driver. No respect. No concern for children. I had a pretty good guess which one it was, too.

"I guess you're old enough now. But I hope you understand, you'll always be my *baby*, no matter how old you get."

More staring. Her eyes looked so sad, so tired.

I took a deep breath and told her the rest. Well, most of it, anyway. How my mom had killed herself. The rape, the promises Marvin made, his smacks and threats. I tried not to spend too much time on the bad and violent parts, because she'd always be my little girl. I wanted to fill her head with happy, good stories, like Dorothy's adventures in OZ with her magical ruby slippers and colorful friends.

I didn't get into the part about how many times I'd almost died—mostly because of her father—but also how I'd nearly killed myself from not eating, even though that was part of why Jenny cheered me up with thoughts of a baby.

My daughter had saved me before she was even born.

I also skipped over how close Delilah came to getting aborted or not surviving her difficult birth.

Instead, I told her how Jenny wasn't ready to be a mom at that time, but knew how much I wanted to be one, and how we came up with this plan to keep ourselves safe and as far away from Marvin as possible, and how we'd tricked the people in the hospital into putting my name on her birth certificate.

I tried to make it sound like a wonderful adventure, where Jenny and I cared about her so much—even before she was born—that we'd do ANYTHING to make sure she came out okay and had the best possible chance at a happy childhood. *Much different than the ones we had*—I thought but didn't say. I wanted her understanding but not her pity. Never any pity.

Delilah listened, staring at me with her big beautiful eyes. I couldn't quite read her expression. She didn't look as angry as when she first started to demand answers. More like concentrating hard, like when she was working on a difficult homework problem. After I got done, I asked if she had any questions.

"Can I call her? My real mom?"

Her words *real mom* felt like a slap, worse than so many real slaps in my life. I took a deep breath, and pointed out that it was already very late in Tennessee. But she could call the next morning.

After that phone call, she said something that felt even worse, almost knocking me to the ground.

"I want to go live with them in Tennessee."

I had to let her go. If I didn't she would resent me forever, or leave anyway when I wasn't looking.

I held it together, trying to be strong, saying things like, "I love you so much," and "I'm so proud of you" and "Call me if you need anything" and I tried to stay calm, even though I felt so... angry at the cab driver. Angry at Jenny for taking away my baby. Reneging on those promises of so many years ago. I couldn't be angry at my beautiful girl, looking so grown up all of a sudden in her nice pink blouse and slacks and good, comfortable shoes, with her suitcase and airplane ticket.

I kissed her goodbye and held it together as she waved at me one last time before she disappeared into the jetway. I held it together as they closed the door and the plane pulled away from the gate. I said a little prayer that the small and fragile-looking airplane would make it safely to the mainland. While the plane lifted off, I took a deep breath and inhaled the scent of plumeria leis. That's when I lost it. So many memories flooded back all at once. The first time I came to

Hawaii, not much older than she was now. The time I took that flight to Newfoundland after my mom died.

I cried so hard there at the window, looking out onto the runways, that I ran out of tissues and handy-wipes in my purse. I hid in a nearby bathroom stall, blowing my nose with toilet paper.

I'd wanted my baby to have a better life than me. But here she was leaving home way too early. I had no idea if Jenny could take care of her well. She had a husband, but I'd never met him. What if he was just as bad as Marvin? Why had she been asking me for my Social Security number? What kind of shady schemes were they dreaming up over there?

It's not like Delilah could just get on a bus or hitch a ride home like I'd done so many times in my youth.

Had she chosen to leave because she was mortified and embarrassed and ashamed—like I had been when I decided to leave? Had I driven her to a fate not so different from my own, even though I'd tried so hard to do the exact opposite?

I cried so hard in that airport bathroom that a nice lady asked, "Are you okay in there?"

"I'm okay, thank you." I was NOT okay, but I wiped off my face, flushed the toilet, washed my hands and smiled weakly at the nice lady.

I had to get back to work. Airplane tickets to the mainland weren't cheap and I needed to have enough savings so she could come home anytime or I could go get her or... I didn't know. At least work would keep me distracted from missing my baby.

Chapter Twenty-Six

Delilah the Teen

One day a letter came in the mail, and I recognized Delilah's handwriting immediately. Why would she be sending me a letter?

I ripped it open.

Dear Mom,

I'd never been so happy to see three letters: MOM. I was still her Mama.

I'm so sorry...

She went on to tell me how her so-called stepdad might have the phone tapped so she was afraid to call me and tell me how miserable she was there, how she wanted to come home, how she loved her biological mom but I was her REAL mom, Hawaii was her REAL home, and could she please please please come home?

My body couldn't decide whether to laugh or cry. I did a little happy dance right there in the lobby by the mailboxes. I zipped up to our apartment and got on the phone to make all the arrangements. My baby was coming home!

This time, I'd fly to Tennessee myself, just to make sure nothing went wrong. No way was I going to let them try anything funny or keep my child a moment longer.

When I finally got there and had her in my arms I squeezed her so tight she finally said, "Mom, I love you but I can't breathe."

The whole trip home she told me how sorry she was and how she'd never leave me again and how much she missed me. My heart overflowed and my cheeks started to hurt from smiling so much.

Of course, my dear sweet Delilah was growing up too fast, and started to notice boys. They noticed her, too. I had to lay down more rules. I kept them simple, like NO (straight) BOYS IN OUR HOME.

One evening, I came home for just a minute to change clothes and grab some more handi-wipes. I had a co-worker friend with me, thank God for that small blessing. When we first came in, I noticed some unfamiliar keys on the bookshelf next to the front door. I caught the scent of cigarette smoke, and noticed butts in a make-shift ashtray on the coffee table. The sound from my big screen TV hit me—cheesy music—and I saw naked people. Porn!?

I charged into Delilah's room, grabbed the young man in there with her by the hair and the back of his shirt, and shoved him out the front door.

He started to protest, "I need my key—"

The door slammed in his face. I locked it, and charged back into her room.

Kris sat, eyes wide. At least they still had all their clothes on. But what if I didn't happen to come home at just that moment?

"Mom, we weren't—"

"You know the rules."

"But I—"

"No buts!" Rage built in me and my friend stood next to me, watching us like a tennis match.

"That's not fair!" She stood up and glared at me.

"Honey, life's not fair."

"Why'd you have to embarrass me in front of him, he's not—"

"You CHOSE to break the rules."

"The rules are bullshit!"

"Watch your language, young lady."

She turned to leave the room. I grabbed her arm to stop her.

"Fucked up, bullshit-ass rules!"

My other hand came up to her face almost in slow motion, all on its own. The loud slap shocked both of us. Her wide eyes filled with tears, her cheek turning red.

"Bitch!" she shouted, and my friend caught my hand before I could swing again.

"Maria," my friend said, looking me right in the eyes. "That's your little girl."

I let go of Delilah. She ran into the bathroom and slammed the door shut.

My friend touched my back gently and led me to the living room. "It's okay, it's all over now."

I dropped onto the sofa, all sorts of violent memories swirling in my head. I'd promised myself I would never, ever hit my kid. I wanted to keep her safe from any harm. *That's what the rules are for.* But then I did it myself. I buried my face in my hands. I wanted to tell her *I'm sorry, I didn't mean it, it'll never happen again.* But I didn't think it would ever happen in the first place. Had I become a monster like all those who caused me harm?

The next day, the young man's mother came for his keys because he was too terrified to come back. Delilah didn't speak to me for days.

Chapter Twenty-Seven

California

Not so long after I scared away Delilah's late-night date, I met a guy who seemed to love me for who I was, despite my past and two previous marriages. He was a super-handsome marine. He made me feel beautiful and special, and was good with Delilah.

She wasn't so crazy about him, but she wasn't crazy about anyone those days.

My new guy got a transfer to move back to the mainland—to Camp Pendleton in California. Right on the beach. "Come with me," he said, when he got the orders. So handsome, so charming, with brown eyes that looked so deep into me, offering to take me away.

"But my daughter, she needs to finish school, and—"

Almost as though he read my mind, he said, "We'll get married. Be a real family. The military has great benefits."

When I hesitated, he said, "You can quit this life for good... just be a wife and mom."

I didn't say anything, thinking it over. He held my hand and touched my cheek. I got distracted by his handsome face and twinkly eyes. One of my friends called him *Sergeant Major Heartthrob* when she teased me about him.

"The schools in California are much better. Don't you want your daughter to have the best possible education, and best shot at a good life?"

How could I argue with that?

Delilah found all kinds of ways to argue. Loudly. About moving. About my crappy choice of husband. Why didn't I marry a nice guy like Doug? What if she refused to go? What if, what if...

"What if," I came back, "we have a big, beautiful wedding, and live happily ever after?"

"Mom, you're delusional," she walked away, shaking her head, slamming doors behind her. I had to be optimistic for both of us. Plan our new future, one moment at a time.

I'd be leaving the life and all the big bucks for a quiet, military life in California. So I figured I may as well have that big beautiful wedding I'd never had with those first two husbands.

I found the most gorgeous, fluffy white gown, rented a huge limo, and THE SHOES! So beautiful and not as uncomfortable as you might think. I felt like Cinderella, finally going to the ball with her prince, wearing glass slippers and dancing all night. I ignored Delilah's pouting, determined to have fun blowing the last of the dollars I'd earned from my old life, so I could go enjoy life with Mr. (finally) Right.

When we got to California, my new husband didn't share his military paycheck, or his limited off-duty time, with me and Delilah as much as I'd imagined he would. This didn't make me happy, but I was determined to make my new life work. So I got a couple of jobs on base. One as a bartender where I used all my charms except for the most private. Not nearly as much cash I used to bring in. Uncle Sam took his chunk. I gave Delilah allowance—sometimes, I admit, to get her to complain less. That left very little for me.

Working all those jobs took a toll, and soon I landed in the hospital, again. When they did finally locate my new husband—who was already cheating on me—he'd forgotten the "in sickness and in health" promise.

Delilah came to my side, and sat quietly with me, looking so sad. In this military hospital, so sterile but bright, I'd lost track of how many times I'd almost died. This time, one of my damaged girl parts finally exploded. Felt like my own body was punishing me for my life and my choices, making me question why I was still alive after all of this, after so much had happened to me. So much bad, so much violence, and now another betrayal—this man I'd loved and trusted, a man I'd thought was the one. I'd shared with him all my secrets and fears. I realized too late that this was my pattern. I'd shown him the blueprint to my heart. How to make me feel loved despite my past. And here he just used it to get what he wanted for me, all my money and the best sex he'd ever had, and he tossed it away when another girl came around.

Delilah brought snacks and flowers to the hospital and listened to the doctors and nurses as they told me how lucky I was to be alive. I didn't feel lucky, except for having Delilah, sitting there beside me even though I'd dragged her across the Pacific, away from her friends and her life in Hawaii.

She never did say, *I told you so.*

When I told her she was right, I was done with his lying and cheating bullshit, and going back to Hawaii, she said something even worse than *I told you so*. She said, "I'm not going with you."

She'd met her own handsome soldier, and how could I possibly argue with her about any kind of choice of boyfriend or husband? Also, she was nearly an adult. Trying to put up a fight would only damage our relationship even more. I had no choice but to let her go.

Chapter Twenty-Eight

Back in Hawaii

When I returned to Hawaii, without my daughter, at least I was finally also without a pimp. Even after Marvin passed away, I hadn't been completely free of a pimp, until I actually moved away with my new husband. That short-lived so-called love of my life may as well have been a pimp for all the money I spent on our wedding, and the zero dollars he ever contributed. Worse—he stole my heart and my confidence that I'd ever find love.

At least that last pimp I had—along with most of the girls in Waikiki—only took some of my money for a little bit of so-called protection. Not that I couldn't take care of myself. And not that his protection didn't keep one of my friends and coworkers from getting thrown off a high floor. And another from getting dismembered.

They identified her by her head.

I tried to shove the terror and fear and grief down deep so I could get on with my life. Didn't work well. I ignored my feelings the way the world ignored me and my peers. We almost always got overlooked by society, the press, and the courts. Many considered us disposable. Garbage. They wanted to pretend we didn't exist.

For my friend who got beheaded—the cops knew who did it. We all did. I didn't sleep well at night for years, kept getting flashes of her severed head. Ran scared when I'd see him walking free.

All the girls who were murdered, died at their own hand of drug overdoses and other forms of suicide, or just disappeared never to be seen again, could fill so many books.

The one time that the press DID pay any attention—with a big full-color spread in a big-time local magazine—my lawyer friend called me about it and asked, "What are you doing talking to the press?"

"What article?" I had no idea what he was talking about, hadn't seen it. There were so many personal details that very few people would know, he'd assumed they'd come from me.

When I got my hands on it... I was horrified. The details shared, about how a few of us girls were advertising and where we were doing our business, could help the cops easily bust us if they wanted, or at least make our lives a lot more difficult. I'd managed to stay out of prison since that first awful 40 days in Rikers. This freedom was thanks to friends I'd made (or paid) to help keep me safe, and all those wigs and sunglasses.

Worse than the unwanted press—I was pretty sure which close, now FORMER, friend had betrayed me by sharing all the details of my life that were nobody's business.

Luckily, I had a lot of nice customers then, some I actually enjoyed spending time with. In another life, another situation, I might've been friends with some of them. One john comes to mind at certain times, when I see Pez candy, and one of the many Outrigger hotels in Waikiki.

My first workplace on 42nd Street across from the Port Authority in New York—with those disgusting sheet-covered plywood beds—was a long way from my post-California haunts in Waikiki. A lot of miles, a lot of years, and too much experience.

This strip of land so popular with tourists and locals, where I built my home and a life for my daughter, wasn't so different from Manhattan in a lot of ways. Both are full of colorful, weird, wacky, and lonely people, looking for love and some kind of escape from reality for a few weeks, days, or just minutes.

Right in the middle of Waikiki, sits an Outrigger Hotel near Prince Edward Street which some of the other girls used to call "Prince Albert Street" as a joke. I've seen more than my share of Prince Albert-style penis piercings but those aren't the men that stick out most in my memory.

These days, when I see Pez candy dispensers, I think of one john who came from far-away and much colder Canada. My old motherland. He was a lovely older Canadian man I'll call Peter. He was a regular to Hawaii's working girls since forever. For each of his two yearly visits, he'd stay for a week and see someone every day. He started asking for just me (yay!) because of my Canadian roots. I made him laugh and he liked my curves. He couldn't actually do anything (double yay) because he couldn't get it up due to some medical issues. He mostly liked to talk, so we'd just go out for dinner. Compared to the younger girls, I could have an adult conversation with him.

Several years after his twice-a-year visits became exclusive to me, I knocked on his door which was always the same, 1712 at the Outrigger. He opened it and his face lit up. I liked how his saggy wrinkled face would transform when he smiled. He kissed me on the cheek and said, "So good to see you, gorgeous." His gentle hand on my back guided me into the room. He closed the door behind me then stood in front of me—now with his hands holding my arms against me like I was some delicate painting he might hang on the wall and stare at all day.

"What's up, Peter?" I second-guessed my choice of words right away. Nothing was usually *too* "up" with him. "You look especially mischievous today." I almost said *frisky*.

"You are so clever and observant. I've always loved that about you," he said, guiding me over to the one chair in the room. Lots of guys would shout "I love you!" in the heat of the moment. Others would say "I love you" after, especially the younger ones who'd never had sex before. This was the closest Peter had ever come to saying he loved me. What the heck was going on?

"You're too sweet Peter. Everything okay? Talk to me, honey." I sat down in the palm-tree-print chair that matched the curtains and tried to read his face. Normally we'd start our visit sitting side-by-side on the bed.

His words came out in a rush. "You know how I have a hard time... I mean because of my diabetes I can't always..."

I'd never seen his soldier stand at attention, but that was fine by me. "It's no big deal, Sweet—"

"No, that's the thing, the doctors gave me this new shot and I didn't want to try it until I was here, with you."

I felt special and a little mortified at the same time. "Aww, that's sweet, Peter. So, no dinner first?"

His hands went to his face. "Oh I'm so sorry, and here you're all dressed up so nice."

I was mostly messing with him. Refreshing how soon he jumped to *sorry*, and stalled so easily. He only glanced at the new red dress

I'd bought. His stare stopped at the cleavage I'd carefully arranged for him.

"You like my new dress? I got this new lacy bra, too." Both bright red. I pulled back a little of the v-neckline to give him a peek. I'd had my nails painted the same color. That was more for me than him.

"Oh, you're killing me," he said.

His goofy grin took decades off his age.

"We can go to dinner later, I was just messing with you. Tell me about this new drug."

"Well it's a shot, kind of like the diabetes drugs I take, but it's supposed to fix my... you know... hard-on thing, in just a matter of minutes. Sounds like too good to be true but the doctor said it works for some people so I was hoping, thinking if anyone could possibly help me with this it would be you."

"So what are you waiting for then, try it out! I want to see what happens." Part of me did, most of me didn't.

"Really?' he asked, like I just told him it was OK to open a Christmas present a day early or something.

"Of course."

He dashed off before I had a chance to say anything else.

I got up and walked over to the sliding glass door, meaning to close the palm-tree-print curtains, but instead I stepped out into the humid air. Would this be a new chapter with my dear favorite customer, Peter? Would I have to pull the stunts I normally pulled with the tourists so he wouldn't ever have actual sex with me? I hoped not. I didn't want to have to do that to him after all these years of his trying. The guilt would weigh on me. I really hoped the shot didn't work.

"OK!" he called out, walking back into the room. "Where did you go?" His voice sounded scared like I'd ditched him or something. I stepped back in and closed the door behind me and the curtains just in case.

"I'm right here, darling. How are you doing?" I said.

He stood there wearing just a white short-sleeved dress shirt like you see the bicycling Mormons. Besides that, he had nothing on except for his white socks. His dick hung limp. As usual. Pointing at the floor. He looked a bit helpless yet hopeful, peering down at himself and then up at my cleavage.

"Well, let's see what happens here." My turn to guide him over to sit on the bed. I flipped back the bedspread. I heard things about how often those bedspreads were washed or not, like never, and my inner clean freak didn't even want his naked butt cheeks sitting on any of that possible nastiness. I pulled my dress over my head in one swift motion, and his eyes went wide at my near-nakedness, even though he'd seen me so many times before.

"Oh I missed you so much, it's so good to see you again."

Now he had his right hand on his little soldier and his left hand on the ladies. I reached around to unhook the new bra. He said, "Wait, don't do that, I just want to... I just want to look at them for a minute, they're so beautiful, you're so beautiful..."

This was pretty much his usual pattern. I leaned back and made noises like I was enjoying his fondling. I spread my legs open a little like you see in the pornography shots for Playboy magazine pictures, trying my best to match the images the world tells men are sexy. Still no soldier standing at attention—just laying there.

"Do you want me to try?" I asked.

"Ok." This was different than our usual. I pulled and tugged and did my best, but before we got him too raw, and before he looked too sad... I started to sing the closing song from the old TV show "Sha na na." I hoped this would make him laugh. "Goodnight, sweetheart, well, it's time to go." Half a smile.

"Yeah," he said, "time to go to dinner. What do you feel like tonight?"

The next night of that same visit, I knocked on the door, same time, same room, same... silence? His usual cheerful greeting was missing. I knocked on the door a little louder. "Peter?" Still nothing. I checked my watch in case I'd somehow messed up the time. Nope. The hairs on my arms stood up. I tried the door.

It opened.

Peter, on his back, fully dressed, rested on the made bed. I eyed the nasty bedspread for a second until I noticed he wasn't sleeping, his eyes were wide open and his mouth was foaming a little and his throat was working, trying to swallow his own tongue!

"Oh my god, Peter, are you okay?" I shook his shoulders but his eyes just stared into nothing. I put my ear to his chest. Still breathing. I glanced at the phone, didn't really want to call hotel security, HE wouldn't want this favorite hotel knowing what was going on in his favorite room 1712.

I tried to pull apart his mouth but it was locked, like a rottweiler that grabbed onto something. I couldn't get it open. He couldn't talk and tell me what was wrong. Maybe I could fix this myself. Maybe he'd just forgotten to take his diabetes medicine. That might be it. I went into his bathroom. He had two different kinds of shots. One for the diabetes, the other his new medicine for play time. But which was which? Why didn't they label these things better?

I had a 50/50 shot. Better than Vegas.

If I did get the wrong one, that play time shot didn't do nothin' anyway. I picked one and went back into the bedroom. He looked the same. I wasn't sure where to stick it. In the movies, when someone overdoses, you see them shoot it right in their heart. Peter never took any of those kinda drugs. I picked the biggest muscle I could see, his thigh. I took a deep breath and shot it in there.

I willed him to sit up, blink and wipe that nasty foam off his mouth, smiling that big smile that lit up his whole face.

Nothing.

I put my ear to his chest again. Was his breathing more shallow? Had I made it worse? Did I just kill my favorite customer? I couldn't avoid calling for help any longer. I picked up the phone and tapped 0.

"Aloha, front desk."

"I need medical help, it's... my Dad..." Didn't want to mess up anyone's reputation.

"I'll send security, and an ambulance, is he breathing?"

"Yeah, but he's kinda choking."

"Okay, security's on the way."

I hung up the phone. *I'm going to be the hooker known for killing her customer.*

Out of habit or nervousness, or watching too many crime TV shows, I started wiping everything down in case they dusted for prints if he died. I didn't know what I was doing. I never should've given him that shot, I kept telling myself, over and over as a wiped and looked at him and waited.

After FOREVER, the security guy came and tried the same thing I did, trying to move that tongue but it was all big. Finally the paramedics came. One checked him over while the other shot questions at me. He asked me a second time: "You gave him *this* shot?" His eyes stared through me.

"Yes, I didn't know, I thought—"

"He needed sugar, not a shot." His words dripped with disgust. "You could've killed him."

I covered my face, holding tears down. Sucked in a breath and peeked through my fingers.

The other paramedic gave his peer a hard look and told me, "You didn't kill him. *That* shot doesn't do squat. He just needed some sugar."

I let out a breath and choked down a chuckle. Later we might joke about what kind of sugar he really needed. If there was a later.

They put him on a gurney and prepared to haul him away.

"You're the daughter?" the nicer one asked. Took me a second to remember the lie I'd told.

"Right."

"Did you want to ride with him in the ambulance?"

I did but I didn't. Part of me wanted to hold his hand and be there when he came out of it. Another part wanted to flee. "I better follow in the car so I can take him home later." That sounded good, right?

"Ok, we're taking him to Queens."

"Right. Queens." I wanted to make sure he was okay, but... I also had the urge to flee not just this room but the island. In case he didn't wake up. Had to make more money right now if I was going to run. But I couldn't run. What about my pets? Where would I run to on this island, anyway? Crazy.

The next day I showed up again at the usual time, hoping he'd answer the door like normal. I knocked. Silence. I should've called the hospital. Gone there to make sure he was okay. I should never have... Wait, what was that sound?

The door swung open.

"Hey, there's my gorgeous gal!" His face looked paler than normal, but at least he was alive.

I hugged him hard. "I'm so glad you're okay, I was worried."

"Yes, the nice ladies at the hospital said 'my daughter' saved my life." He chuckled, holding my face in his hands.

"I didn't know what to do... I'm so glad you're okay, and sorry I didn't go to the hospital, I was afraid they'd check my ID or..." Sorry for so many things.

"Don't worry about it, all good now."

The next year when he came into town, he had another "fix" for his hard-on situation. He showed me the little pamphlet that came with it, small with a bunch of tiny printing in a few different languages.

"So, you had this put in already?" I asked him after looking over the small illustration and reading some of the words. The before and after cartoons reminded me of what my daughter had shown me they were using to teach sex education, lessons that would've been helpful to *me* when I was younger.

They should let ME teach them classes. I chuckled at the thought.

"What's funny?" he asked.

"Just the pictures. They remind me of those big one-legged air dancer things you see outside car dealerships." Instead of a bright color, the picture was white with a black outline. "You know the ones I'm talking about?" I moved my arm to demonstrate. Like really bad hula.

He smiled. "Yes, can you imagine a pee-pee that tall?"

I didn't have to imagine, I'd had nightmares like that. And a customer or two who'd come close. But I wasn't going to share *those* stories with him. I also didn't ask why he used the word "pee-pee." That's what they DO (and all I could think about when I first started) not what they were called. And I'd heard so many names for penises like "Big Joe" or "Little Joe" on a guy named Joe. Or anaconda banana... like some kind of song. On a subconscious level his man parts maybe didn't like being called a "pee pee" and refused to stand at attention. How many times have I thought *I could've been a shrink.*

This new gadget wasn't going to work, was it?

"Should we try it?" I asked.

He nodded eagerly and pulled down his pants. Outside, the band playing nearby launched into an old ABBA song. "Just a second," I jumped up and opened the sliding door wider to hear better. Stalling. "I love this song."

"Should we request a drum roll?" he smiled.

"You're so funny." I looked at the situation down below. The picture had an arrow to where the small button would be, under the skin. His scrotum area had much more fur than the pamphlet illustration, so I had to poke around, gently, until I felt the button. "Ready?"

"Yes, ma'am!"

I pressed it, and his dick moved up. Like a lever. No change in size, just a change in direction. Like it was pointing over there then over here. Almost like those John Travolta moves from the 70s.

His brow furrowed. We both expected... more.

"That's *ALL*?" he asked.

I let go of the button. Pete Junior dropped back into his usual resting position.

"I mean, I didn't expect fireworks or confetti to pop out of it but..."

I held back a giggle. Confetti would've been fun. He looked so disappointed, and on the verge of tears. I took a gamble that I could make him laugh.

"You can dance!" the cover singer belted out.

I pressed the button again, up/down, moving it in time to the music and sang along, "You can jive!"

He looked down, his eyebrows still scrunched together. Half a smile.

"You should name him 'John Travolta'" I suggested, pointing it this way and that with the music.

"Having the time of your life!" the lady outside sang.

"He could have his own disco show."

Peter shook his head and laughed.

I pictured a John Travolta Pez Dispenser. Was there such a thing?

Peter's laughing turned to hiccups and I wondered if there was a shot for that. I brought him a glass of water and rubbed his back.

"Oh well." He said between hiccups. "What will they think of next?"

Chapter Twenty-Nine

The Red Light Ladies

The year I started writing this book, I turned 50, and on the outside, I had it all: a two-bedroom condo in Hawaii, just a couple of blocks from the beach, a beautiful white Jaguar, flexible hours (I worked when I wanted because I was my own boss), and my sweet dogs Bella and Sophia. I missed my daughter. She now had a daughter of her own! Although they lived on the mainland, I saw them pretty often.

Still, I felt like a walking corpse. Dead inside. I couldn't keep doing this job forever. My multiple surgeries caught up to me, like the breast augmentations that now caused back pain. Most days I'd put on a happy face, joke with my friends and tourists out on the street, even come home with a pile of money, but I wanted to cry. When the tears did leak out, Bella and Sophia would lick them off my face and look at me like, *Don't cry Mom, it'll be okay.*

Out there on the streets while trying to make a living, I'd sometimes see The Church Ladies. That's what my friends and I called them because they looked like they were coming from church with their slacks and long dresses, and talk of God. They tried so hard to have conversations with us. Usually I was the first to flee. But one night, this tiny Japanese lady who often looked scared-to-death, stared me right in the eyes and asked me my name.

"Maria, that's what my friends call me, anyway."

I saw her glance at the small gold cross I often wore on a chain around my neck.

"But my real name is Mary." I was surprised I volunteered this to a complete stranger. "What's your name, sweetheart?"

"Uh... Mona," she said. Not sure of her own name? "Actually, it's just Claire."

I looked at her, hard, about to ask, when she blurted out an answer.

"One of the other ladies thought we shouldn't use our real names out here..." she trailed off, looking around at all the tourists, street performers, military guys, and vendors selling trinkets. I doubted she came to Waikiki much, if ever. Did she want to pretend to be someone she wasn't to be more like us? Or practice sinning? I had no idea why they lied. I tried to remember if "don't lie" was one of the 10 Commandments. A tiny white lie for a tiny lady.

She cleared her throat, moving on. "I noticed you're wearing a cross." She saw her chance.

I touched the cross and thought of Nana. Mona-Claire reminded me of her.

"Maria!" I heard my name called from down the block. A girl that I sometimes worked with, called my name again.

"I gotta go, Claire, nice to meet you." I ran off and joined her, forgetting all about The Church Ladies for a while.

A few weeks later, on a busy Saturday night on Kuhio street, near the Denny's, I saw Claire again. "Maria." She smiled and clutched some brochures, looking nervous but not as scared as last time.

"Hi, beautiful." I touched her arm. She smiled bigger. "Claire, right? Out here again?" I almost added, *Selling Jesus?* We were all selling something. I could hear Nana's voice in my head saying *Don't be wise*.

She nodded, and looked at my cross again. "You know Jesus loves you, right?"

"Sure."

"And God has a plan for you?"

I glanced at my cell phone to check the time, a top-of-the-line Blackberry.

"I have to go Claire, nice to see you."

"Here, take this." She pressed one of her brochures into my hand before I fled. I smiled.

When I got home and settled into my favorite comfy yellow chair, surrounded by my dogs, I pulled out my purse to count my cash. I found Claire's brochure in my purse, folded in half. Claire's church was in Kaneohe, the Windward side of O'ahu. The pamphlet showed huge glass windows so you could see the lush green mountains, with ribbons of white here and there. Waterfalls. They must've taken the pictures after a good rain.

My nosey dog Bella sniffed the paper. "When's the last time we were over on the Windward side, Bell?"

The images of the church called to me. But I had mortgage payments to make and the lease on my Jaguar, and dog treats to buy. I put Claire and God and the beautiful church out of my mind. I had to put everything out of my head in order to do the work I hated more each day. I felt empty, like a husk of a human.

One night, I saw Claire again but really didn't want to talk to her. She just seemed too sweet, though, like she really wanted to help me. Like God was truly right here in her heart. He might not've been anywhere else in the dark underbelly of Waikiki, but God was there, in Claire. He had to be. I needed him to be.

She saw me, smiled so big I thought I'd cry, and opened her mouth to say something.

I held up my hand to stop her and looked over her shoulder like I saw someone I knew. "I have to run," I lied, feeling sick, choking back a sob. I squeezed her shoulder. "But don't give up on me, Claire." The last part came out in a whisper. I did have to run before I burst into tears.

Later that night, I wandered the streets a bit, not headed anywhere. I didn't feel like chatting with the late-shift Denny's servers I usually joked around with. Didn't have the energy to drum up business. I knew I had to make some money but I just couldn't do it.

Finally, I wandered into the small health clinic near my condo where I usually just grabbed the free condoms. The woman behind the counter looked up from her magazine and right into my eyes.

With a sweet southern drawl, she asked, "You okay darlin'?" Reminded me of Cherry.

The tears came flooding out. I collapsed into one of the chairs in the reception area, my head in my hands. "No, I'm not."

The nice people at the health clinic helped me get some counseling and psych meds. Physically I was fine. In the best shape of my life, working out at the gym regularly. I had a solid core, six-pack abs, which helped strengthen my much-needed back muscles.

I went to Claire's church. And then I went again. I hid in the back as much as possible, then snuck out early before all the coffee and cookies and whatnot they invited everyone to after the service. I liked the singing and the music. Even the preacher was nice to listen to. Much better than the churches I remember Nana liked with all the kneeling my knees probably couldn't have handled anymore. The preacher didn't seem so… preachy. Or bossy. Just telling some personal stories and a few from the Bible that made me think about what it means to be a human on this earth, with just one life, and the choices we make every day about who we are and how we treat each other.

Headed home in my white Jaguar, I'd make the beautiful drive through the lush green Koʻolau mountain range, the Pali tunnel, the roads wet with fresh rain. Often a rainbow in the distance. And I felt something I hadn't in a long time: hope.

Meanwhile, I had bills to pay. I'd cut back on my usual wallet lifting—thou shalt not steal and all that. These guys in Waikiki looking for love or at least a little attention were going to find it eventually somewhere. May as well be *my* bills they helped pay.

The counselor I'd met through the health clinic got me started with the process of getting help from the state. I felt silly about the idea of taking handouts when I could make more money in one night than the state would give me for a whole month on welfare. And I felt ashamed.

So I returned to Claire's church, hoping for something, I didn't know what. A lady stopped me before I could fly out the back, and asked how I'd learned about the church.

"Claire invited me." I explained, wanting to flee but not wanting to be rude.

"Claire.... What's her last name?"

I didn't know her last name. Wasn't sure I'd gotten her real name right.

"They go to Waikiki on Saturday nights," I looked at this woman, waiting for her to figure it out. I half expected she'd blurt out, *Oh, you're a hooker!* Or at least look at me differently.

"Oh, our Red Light Ladies, yes, I know which Claire you mean, I just saw her. Come with me." She slipped her warm soft hand into mine, and pulled me through a whirlwind of people.

Claire was setting out cookies in the back of a room with kids' art adorning the walls.

"Claire, look who I found, hiding in the back, about to sneak out."

"Busted," I said, guilt weighing on me.

"Oh! Mary! You made it." She gave me a big hug. Then she took off the purple orchid lei she wore and put it over my head giving me another hug and a peck on the cheek. "Welcome. I'm so glad to see you, mahalo for coming."

"Thank you for inviting me. I love the music."

"Oh! We have something for you," she looked around trying to remember. "I meant to give it to you before but you always dash off so fast. I'll be right back. Stay here."

I looked at Claire's friend and said with a straight face, "Sometimes I'm kinda fast." I winked at her and she laughed. "It's my job, and the boys like it."

The friend giggled, blushing a little.

"Probably not a lot of fast girls in this joint, huh?"

She looked thoughtful. "Well, you may be surprised. We're all sinners, after all."

The way she said "after all" reminded me of "It's a small world," the ride in Disneyland, where I'd taken my daughter when she was a kid. "A world of laughter a world of *fears*"? That didn't seem right.

The friend looked lost in her own thoughts. Thinking of her own sins? Which of the others had sins similar to mine?

"Okay, here you go." Claire came back, holding a small Hawaiian-print bag with a drawstring at the top. "It's not much but the Red Light Ladies put these together hoping they might—" she handed me the bag and didn't seem to know what to do or what to say— "help a little." She pressed her hands together, prayer pose. I hugged her. Harder than I'd hugged anyone in a long time.

"Thank you so much, Claire. This is too sweet."

The two friends smiled at each other. More people filed into the room, headed for the cookies and coffee. "I do have to run, though, my dog Bella needs her medication."

"Oh!" Claire looked like she was about to ask what kind of dog or tell me she loved dogs, so I blew them both a kiss.

"Thank you, again." I held up the gift bag and dashed for my car, hoping lightning wouldn't strike me down for telling a lie to these nice ladies right in a church building. Bell didn't need no medication. She was my medication.

After Claire found out I was going to church, she looked for me on Sundays and I even gave her my cell phone number. Eventually, she asked me to meet the pastor. I wasn't so sure about any of this. I almost canceled the meeting with the pastor, since part of me felt like that time way back in elementary school when I got sent to the principal's office. The pastor often talked about not judging others, but we're all human. How could he not judge or at least have some sort of opinion about my life. Would he throw me out of his church before I corrupted the nice, innocent people? Should I put off the meeting for a while so I could still enjoy the church before they kicked me out? I wouldn't feel comfortable if I did, not knowing and stalling might make me more nervous. Would he forgive me like he talked about during his sermons? How could I explain all I'd been through?

I came up with an idea to save me some talking. I already had some chapters of this book written, so I printed out what I had and brought it with me to the meeting.

Claire led me to his office from the entrance to the church. He smiled so warmly and gave me the plumeria lei he wore, a big hug, and a peck on the cheek. "Aloha, Mary, so great to meet you. Claire has told me all about you."

I glanced at Claire, wondering what she'd said. She just smiled.

"Well not ALL about me, 'cuz she doesn't know all of it," I said, touching my handbag where I'd stashed the print-out.

"Sure, just the important parts—how you're a beautiful soul and you know God loves you."

I could feel my face flush. Not like me, I never blushed. What was it about these people that made me feel like I was a kid again? Back before Mom died and everything turned to crap.

I looked down, took a deep breath, inhaling the scent of the plumeria lei, reminded of my first time to Hawaii.

"Thank you for the lei. I have something for you, too." In a moment of bravery–or foolishness, not sure which–I pulled out the pages and held them, curled, in my hands, like a piece of pipe. I squeezed it for a second, fighting my sudden urge to flee.

"That's so kind of you," he said, urging me on, holding his hands out.

I opened the roll and slowly put it on his hands, flat, with my hand on top. Not quite ready to let go. I held the hand sandwich. Or paper sandwich, with hands for bread.

"This is who I am," I said, one word at a time, before I got too distracted by my own thoughts of sandwiches.

"Oh, that's your book!" Claire gushed, looking a little jealous. Maybe I should have brought two copies. But sharing this story with even one other person was hard enough.

As I hesitated letting go, the pastor said, "I'm honored, and humbled, that you would share this with me."

I held on a second more. "This is me. If you're okay with who I am, then..." I let it go.

He held the papers to his chest. "Thank you so much."

"If you're okay with all that, then..."

He gave me one more hug. He could probably tell I was about to burst into tears. I was trying to say, "Then I'm okay with you." But I didn't get that far.

I stepped back and mumbled. "I have to go." I turned to Claire, "Thank you, thank you both." Then I was outta there. Not sure what I had just done.

Chapter Thirty

In Her Shoes

Another Christmas season rolled around, and the only way we knew was because Waikiki was decked out with surfing Santas wearing leis, shorts, and flip-flops or "slippahs," we say in Hawaii. Sometimes I missed the snow in New York. But I'd take a white-sand Christmas over a white Christmas any day. No one would freeze to death in Hawaii.

Sometimes my family would visit around the holidays, but not this time. Too expensive. They'd been here recently, my granddaughter was busy with school and friends. So many reasons and I got it. They had lives of their own now, and I was happy they did. I'd already sent presents to my kid and grandkid. We could still make fun of the surfin' Santas together, just over the phone. I'd text my granddaughter the silliest ones. She'd send back an lol sometimes.

I was actually looking forward to the big Christmas day events planned at the church. I realized how the welcoming people at Claire's church had already given me a huge gift -- some hope about the future.

And a safe place to sit and listen to music and Pastor Don. Some counselors and a psychiatrist I met through the Waikiki health clinic helped me face some of my long-buried demons and my PTSD. Also my ADD. I'd have a better chance of making a plan to get out of my long-time profession–and sticking to it–if I could focus better. And not cry myself to sleep so much.

But I still had to eat. My dogs did too. Pay the mortgage on my condo and half of the rent on the studio apartment I shared with one other girl, since it was a lot cheaper than renting hotel rooms. I still worked the streets just enough to get by. Although I was starting to let my mortgage payments slip.

The health professionals talked to me about potential jobs I could do instead. Lots in the service industry. They asked me what I liked doing the most and I told them, taking care of kids.

On Christmas Eve, it was just me and my thoughts and my dogs in my condo. I had a DVD a friend of mine had lent me. "I think you'll like this," she said. "It's about dogs. And fashion. And sisters." She knew I loved dogs and my sister. And I liked to shop for nice clothes or purses and especially shoes.

I snuggled up with Bella and Sofia and dropped the DVD into the player. *In Her Shoes* was about two sisters who were very different–made me miss my big sister Vivian. The younger sister in the movie, played by Cameron Dias, was the wild one. A bit like me. Sometimes taking too many chances and getting herself in trouble. I had been wearing my hair blonde lately, like Cameron, and had always had an appreciation for shoes, so the movie had me hooked right away.

As the plot unfolded I realized I had something else in common with these two sisters. Something that the friend who'd lent me the DVD didn't know. They'd also lost their mother to suicide.

I held my dogs closer to me, petting them as I watched the younger sister steal a dog, and the older sister bring him back. I watched them fight how I do sometimes with my sister.

Later in the movie, we meet their grandmother played by Shirley MacLaine. The grandma's calm and wisdom reminded me of my Nana. The movie grandma explains how she knew the sisters' mother death was a suicide, not a car accident, because she'd received a letter the day of the funeral, with just one sentence: "Please take care of my babies."

Then the DVD player stopped. Right then.

After those words:

Take care of my babies.

I sucked in a breath and held it, waiting for the DVD to continue. It didn't. Those were also the last words my mother said before she took her life.

I let out a long breath, listening to the odd silence. Too quiet. Scary and magical at the same time. Why had the DVD stopped just then? The power was still on. The DVD had never done anything like that before.

"It's a sign," I said to Bella. "A sign," to Sophia. They stared back at me. I swear Sophia squinted and nodded the slightest bit.

A message from God.

I didn't dare say that out loud. But I felt it deep down. The silence in the dark room felt like a blanket. Calm. I knew what I had to do now. Quit forever. Take care of babies. No doubt in my mind.

The next day after the beautiful Christmas services, with lots of my favorite songs –I sang louder than ever–Claire found me and this time I didn't run off so fast. I went with her to the refreshments, and made small talk with a few people.

Pastor Don spotted me and came over. I hadn't heard anything from him since I'd handed over the chapters of my book. I knew he was a very busy man, so I didn't know if he'd had a chance to read any of them.

"Mary, so good to see you. Merry Christmas!"

"Thank you, same to you. Beautiful service."

"Thanks. Do you have a minute to chat in private?"

This made me nervous. Not that I minded chatting in private–I trusted him. But why? Did he want to let me down easy? Not embarrass me in front of the rest of the congregation?

I followed him back to his office. The walk felt very long, like I was going to the principal's office, or to my death sentence. What if he kicked me out of the church? I'd be lost again. I needed these people. I couldn't start all over again. How many times had I had to start over again in some new place with all new people and fears to face?

I stayed standing, even though he indicated the chair in front of his desk. I wanted to ask him what he thought, to demand he spit it out already, but at the same time I didn't want to rush my getting kicked out. I held my breath.

"I'm so impressed with you."

I sat down, relieved.

"I'm so impressed, in fact," he took the pages out of a drawer and put them down in front of me. "I want to ask you a favor." I thought he was about to ask me to join Claire and the rest of the Red Light Ladies out on the streets of Waikiki. Instead, he said, "How do you feel about international travel?"

"Uh..." I had no idea where he was going with this. I'd been to Canada a few times, but that was barely international.

"Specifically, the Philippines."

I knew some people from there. That's about it. "I've never been."

"Well then, I hope you'd think seriously about joining a group of us that's going. We want to do some outreach to some young women there who we think might..." he hesitated for a moment, "... benefit from your experience."

I didn't know what to say. When I said nothing, he added, "We'll pay for all your expenses of course."

Now I was really blown away. Here I had hoped he'd let me keep going to his church, and not throw me out for all the terrible things I had done in my past. Instead, he was offering me an all-expenses paid trip! I couldn't believe it.

"That sounds, incredible. I don't know what to say, I—"

"Just say you'll do it!"

"I'd be honored. Yes, I'll do it."

I had no idea how this was going to work. I'd need a passport. I'd need someone to watch my dogs. I needed... I didn't even know. Shots? A visa? A different phone that would work in another country? I had no clue. But at the same time, as Pastor Don smiled at me, I knew that somehow it would all be okay. God was here in this room. He was there in my DVD player the night before. He would make it work somehow.

"Praise God! Thank you, Mary. I can't thank you enough. I know He brought you here for a reason, and as I read your story I could so clearly see that reason."

He tapped the papers in front of me. I rolled them back up and put them away. This time I didn't flee so fast. I asked him a bunch of questions about the when and how and who. He asked me about all my other concerns. He had ideas for every single one of them. Including who might watch my dogs for me. That feeling of dread that had taken over my brain and heart for so long, started to lift.

Chapter Thirty-One

Clicking My Heels Together

My life after that moment with Pastor Don felt like Dorothy's tornado ride to Oz. Such a whirlwind of fear and confusion and excitement all swirled into one hot beautiful mess. Instead of Oz, I landed first in the Philippines, then in Cambodia, a restored pirate ship in Waikiki, a cat sanctuary on the Windward side of the O'ahu, and finally back to the U.S. Mainland.

In my version of the story, the evil witch was all the baggage and trauma from my old life. Even though I had so much joy in my new one—making me want to sing "Ding dong the witch is dead" and "follow the yellow brick road"—bad thoughts, memories, and feelings kept jumping up. It wasn't all just a dream. Although I had plenty of bad ones to fill my head. There were so many times I wanted to click my heels together and be somewhere safe and familiar, like a comfortable loving home. But I wasn't sure what that meant anymore.

I did feel much more at home in church, though, and that was huge.

Fortunately, like Dorothy, I had some excellent companions. First up, the group of people from church that I traveled with to Manila, included a psychiatrist who specialized in PTSD—a huge gift from God, what I needed most at that moment.

I kept thinking of the poem, "Footprints in the Sand." There were sometimes two pairs of footprints and sometimes just one. The poet assumed that was when the Lord left her alone. But those single footprints were actually, as the Lord explained, "When I carried you."

The Lord carried me many times in my years on the streets in different forms. A grumpy New York Irish cop, whisking me away from threats and into safe cabs, like the one driven by my favorite cabby, Doug, who also carried me so many times, keeping me safe and sane. More recently, the Lord carried me through Pastor Don when he baptized me in Waikiki's warm waters off Magic Island, surrounded by Claire and so many other loving souls.

The amazing team from Made In Hope also carried me, raising the money and rounding up the dozen or so people to go on this mission to Manila. They called me Miracle Mary, because it was a miracle I'd survived those many times when I could easily have died or just given up.

When we landed in Manila, I looked around at all the people, quickly assessing them—that old self-preservation habit. All around the city were men with large guns, straps over their shoulder, like the Federales in Mexico. One of the people in our group had mentioned this before we got there during our prep meetings, telling us how ISIS militia were there to recruit young men. They were even in the Mc-

Donalds. Some of the men they spoke to looked more like elementary school kids.

Then I noticed the faces of my own teammates. Many of them looked so scared. Never seen a gun before. Once we got to the busy pre-selected neighborhood, hot and even more humid than Hawaii, I spotted the young working women right away.

One in particular sat on a box, wearing not much more than rags, with her two infants on a flattened box next to her. They wore nothing, not even a diaper. Good thing their skin was pretty dark since they had no protection from the sun at all. They did seem to have some protection from a man on the other side of the street, who watched closely. A man with just one arm. I assumed he was the father of the children and a pimp.

Most of our team, including the very kind psychiatrist, hesitated to approach these women. Not sure if they were scared of the pimps or the nearby armed ISIS recruiters or they just didn't know what to say. I started to cross the street to talk to the mom and the psychiatrist held my arm. "Do you want us to come with you?" So much for all the preparation. Street life was harder than they could imagine.

"No, I got this." And I knew God had me.

Any fear or hesitation didn't come close to my larger urge to help this mama. My plan was to convince her that if I could get out, so could she.

"Hello, do you speak any English?" I asked the reluctant-looking mama, who instinctively put a protective hand on the small children. She stared, confused, and glanced over my shoulder. I said the few words of greeting in Tagalog that I'd recently learned. "Kamusta?" (hello, how are you?). "Ok ka lang?" (are you okay?)

She nodded but kept glancing over my shoulder. I turned to see the one-armed man approaching me. He moved right into my personal space. I pulled back my shoulders, ready to stand my ground.

"Why are you here?" he asked in surprisingly good English.

"I'm just asking if she's okay." That was true, assuming I said the words correctly. I braced for what I expected him to say next.

"You better not show her any disrespect."

That was not what I expected him to say.

"That woman has a master's degree and is very smart."

Also not what I expected. "Wow, that's amazing. Thank you for telling me."

"You show her respect." He looked me up and down, like he was judging me, trying to determine if I believed him.

I nodded. He glanced at the woman, she nodded at him, and he walked away. I let out a breath. My head still spun with the pimp's words. I thought for sure he was going to say something about leaving her alone, that she needed to make money. If I'd had a pimp that spoke up for me like that—I couldn't even imagine.

Once he was gone, I asked again if she spoke English. She shook her head, but said, "No, no English." I told her my story of being on the street, anyway, and selling my body, and how I was able to get out of the life with the help of my friends here. They looked on from across the street. One with a camera.

I could tell the mama was listening, her expression so intent. After a little while, she asked a question in the English she didn't want to admit she knew. "How old is your daughter now?"

"She's all grown up, and has a daughter of her own."

She smiled, and her whole face lit up. I put my hands on either side of her face. "You're so beautiful. You should smile all the time."

Right at that moment, my friend snapped a picture. A few minutes later, he told me the sunlight shown down in a heavenly beam, lighting up both our faces like a miracle had just happened.

I couldn't have imagined how inspiring talking to these women on the streets would be. Such terrible conditions, worse in some ways than Rikers Island had been, yet they held everything together, dedicated to making sure their kids got fed.

Sometimes they didn't know much English at all, and I used mostly hand gestures and drawings to communicate. Our team had a few handouts in various languages which helped us share resources and options available. Many women tucked the pamphlets away, I hoped to look at later.

Back at home, seeing all the pictures from the trip and sharing stories with these churchgoers so dedicated to helping others, I finally felt like this was what I was meant to do. This was why God put me here on Earth.

I had to figure out how to feed myself and my dogs with very little in the way of skills or experience.

Thankfully, the Red Light Angels and others from the church saw strengths in me that I took for granted. They helped me get a job working at a justice restaurant called SEED, which was started to give people like me with difficult pasts including criminal records a chance. At first, I wasn't so sure and I hid in the back, washing dishes and anything else I could do without interacting with the customers. I made lots of jokes and had everyone laughing most of the time. The manager kept telling me, "You should get out front, you're so funny and personable, the customers would love you."

Finally, one day when they were short servers, and partly to keep them from bugging me anymore, I started taking orders. "Fine. Give me one of those notepads. But don't get too mad if I dump food in some laps."

They never got mad at all, even when I did mess up. Turns out free dessert makes everyone happy. I especially loved when families brought their children. Tired parents happily handed over their fussy or crying infants. I'd walk them around the restaurant and the other patrons also appreciated my skills at turning tears into giggles and laughter.

Eventually, SEED shut down, like so many restaurants that fail despite great food and excellent intentions. My new family there had lots of laughter and tears in the final days.

Luckily, my skills with the wee ones didn't go unnoticed. My next job was working at a nursery school in downtown Honolulu, surrounded every day by so much love and cuteness. I had so many struggles finding a new home I could afford, adjusting to no longer being my own boss after so long, and floundering at asking for government help. But all that, and the scars and bad memories from so much trauma in my past life, just washed away when I got to hold a happy baby. The purity and unconditional love. Baby giggles kept me afloat when the weight of real life with hardly any money made me feel like I was about to drown at any moment.

There's one picture of me surrounded by children of all ages, who'd just covered me in stickers. I'm wearing my red-sequin slippers similar to Dorothy's, and I have the biggest smile on my face, sitting there in the middle of all that love and joy. I was home. Finally. I'd clicked my heels together and somehow managed to land right there.

My actual home kept changing based on what the kind people from church could do for me and my pets. For a while, I lived in a cat sanctuary where I could take care of human babies by day, and at night I could help with the four-legged friends—both those who'd been domesticated and those who were wild and free. I could relate to these kitties, since it seemed like I had nine lives or more. I wanted to be free and do what I wanted, be wild like Maria, while also being the more-tame church-going Mary who followed the rules and felt safe in my own skin, sometimes getting a nap in when I could.

Working multiple jobs and scraping together a living left little time for naps and started to take a toll. I missed my daughter and granddaughter—growing up WAY too fast—so after many discussions with my new families in Hawaii, and my family on the mainland, I made a huge decision.

Chapter Thirty-Two

Back to the Mainland

I made the heart-wrenching choice to leave Hawaii—including my cats—to move to California again with my granddaughter, daughter, and her dad in their small home near Sacramento. Delilah's little dog Eddie and my dog Sophia sniffed each other's butts and growled to figure out territory, and they were all best buddies. We humans were not as good at getting along. Some days I couldn't help but think of the 1960s horror flick *What Ever Happened to Baby Jane*.

Fortunately, when things started to get too tense, and COVID travel restrictions loosened up, Sophia and I hit the road to travel and reconnect with some other people on the mainland I hadn't seen in a long time. I was especially grateful to catch up with my sister Vivian, back in Buffalo. Luckily she had more room at her place so we weren't on top of each other so much. I had a room to write and think and remember and recover some. She even gave me an iPad to help me with my writing. We talked about our dreams and joked and laughed almost like when we were innocent girls, before life got so complicated and hard.

Back at my daughter's house, we did get some professional help from counselors to talk through our differences and traumas. But ultimately, I figured it was best for everyone if I went back to Hawaii and gave the kids their space back. I could restart my life doing what I loved most—taking care of little ones.

I was able to get one of my old jobs back, in day care. I had everything packed up and set to go, with the plan to make one more stop to reconnect with an old friend I hadn't seen in a long time. Unfortunately, he'd moved to Las Vegas, a place I hated and never would have returned to if it wasn't for my old friend—my driver and part-time uncle for my little girl, back in the day—Doug.

From the moment I got off the plane and walked through the Las Vegas airport, full of slot machines flashing and blaring, which trigger my PTSD and ADHD, I kept wanting to yell, I hate this place, and sometimes, I FUCKIN' HATE this place. All my nice church friends took a temporary back seat in my head and heart, even though I'd gotten pretty good at not cursing around them. I flashed through a crapload of memories. The first time I came to this horrible place. When I came back to make some money after the bad marine. So many feelings of dread and fear and disgust washed over me. Luckily I had little Sophia with me. She kept kissing me and looking at me with her innocent brown eyes, like she wanted to ask me, "What's wrong, Mom? Why do you hate this place so much?"

I tried to focus on her, her unconditional love and so much sweetness. I held her tightly when she jumped at the sounds from a slot machine we passed. We both had reasons to hate this place.

My old habits—like spotting the cops and potentially dangerous men and other girls who might be working—kicked in and I didn't like it. "We'll be okay," I kept telling Sophia, trying to convince myself. "Doug will be so happy to see us."

Waiting for my bag at the baggage claim, I wondered how much of us he would be able to see, since he'd lost some sight due to diabetes. He lived on the outskirts of Vegas, northeast of the strip, where he'd moved from Hawaii years ago to take care of his parents before they'd passed away.

On the phone while setting up the trip, I'd told him, "You know how much I hate Vegas, right?"

"I know."

"Not too many people I'd go to Vegas to see, you know," I'd said.

"I know. I love you, too."

Doug had a way of cutting through all my bullshit, and even knew what I was trying to say before I could figure out how to say it.

Thankfully, the cab driver who took us to Doug's didn't say too much, leaving me alone with my thoughts. The freeway looked a lot different—bigger, more buildings—yet still the same with the electronic billboards selling sin everywhere you looked.

Sophia shivered in the cold A/C of the cab. We were used to Hawaii, where there were no billboards, and so much more calming things to look at like beautiful green mountains and so many shades of blue skies and ocean.

"Don't worry," I told us both, "we won't be here very long." I heard somewhere the saying about how we humans make plans and God laughs. He must've chuckled a little when I said that to Sophia.

Doug's condo complex was just a couple of miles and a couple of turns off the freeway. There were lots of trees and it felt quieter than the main commercial drag that led there from the freeway. The two-story condos each had an outdoor patio area with high stucco walls—easy to let Sophia out to pee when she needed to go. No high-rises or flashing signs. This didn't feel so much like the rest of Vegas, more like a neighborhood. I breathed a sigh of relief.

The cab driver pulled up to Doug's, unloaded my bag and slammed the trunk shut. I handed him the cash and I bounced Sophia as we stood at the curb, "You ready to see Dougie?"

Doug's patio gate opened, and he stood there in the doorway, holding onto the wall.

"Mary?"

He looked in our direction, with that same warm Doug grin I knew and loved, but he wasn't looking at me. Kind of over my head. He squinted some, into the afternoon sunshine. I moved toward him, "Doug! So good to see you!"

I hugged him hard, kissed him on the cheek and held Sophia up to give him kisses, too. He chuckled. I glanced around the small patio area and noticed some potential hazards, bricks in a pile that could easily trip him if he got off course, the slight step up to the door. Off to my right, peeking down from a cross beam, was a shy back-and-white cat that belonged to... who knew who? She looked right at me. I thought of my kitties back in Hawaii, the ones I'd hoped to see in less than a day. She let out a soft "neee-ow" as though to say, he needs you now. She had no collar and looked thin. They both could use my help.

A warmth like sunlight or a heavy blanket rested on me, God's hand. Stay.

There had been a few special moments in my life when I'd felt God so close to me, telling me what I needed to do, and this was one of them.

"I'm so glad you came." Doug hugged me again. "How long can you stay?" He led me across his small back patio, and reached out for the sliding glass door, missing the handle at first.

I stopped and looked at the chaos in his home and at his face—a little fuller and more wrinkled than the last time I'd seen him, a few more gray hairs, but the same kindness in his eyes.

The ticket in my bag had me on a plane the next day. No way. "I'll stay as long as you need me, Doug. We're here for you."

His shoulders relaxed some and he smiled big. "You are an angel, you know that, right?"

I'd had men call me a lot of things before, but when Doug said kind things to me or about me I knew for sure he really meant it. Why had I wasted so much time with all those other men who said so much they didn't mean?

Inside Doug's home, some stairs to the left led up to a loft area. "The guest suite is upstairs," he told me. "But I'm not sure what's up there."

He struggled to move around. How long had it been since he'd climbed any stairs?

"No worries, Dougie, I'll figure it out."

He smiled at me, and half flopped down onto an off-white double recliner. He looked much more comfortable there, and I figured that was his spot, where he spent most of the hours of his day. "Sweet Mary, you were always so good at figuring everything out."

I sat next to him, on the other side of the double recliner, and held his hand. Sophia jumped down and started inspecting every corner of the cluttered living room.

"I don't know how you did it all. And now Delilah's kid is almost a teenager! Hard to believe."

"I know! You should see that girl." I wanted to pull those words out of the air as soon as I said them since he couldn't see, but instead I kept talking, faster. "Just like Delilah when she was almost a teenager—sassy, smart, always pushing the edge of what she could get away with."

"Hmm, sounds like someone else I know." He squeezed my hand and smiled. Felt like no years or decades had passed, and we were back in Hawaii telling stories about what funny thing had happened to me or Delilah, or some crazy tourist he'd driven around in his cab.

We chatted for hours. Sophia curled up next to me on the recliner and fell asleep.

"I'm sorry, I should've offered you something to eat or drink," Doug started to get up.

"It's okay, sweetie, do you want something? I'll get it."

In his kitchen, I found a couple of glasses, but not much food besides canned goods, junk food and sweets, and a few things in the fridge that were fuzzy. What had he been eating? I didn't know too much about diabetes, but I knew he wasn't supposed to be eating all this crap.

Over the next few days, my mama instincts kicked in for both Doug, who HAD been eating mostly canned and processed food, and the many feral cats, like the one who stared me down that first day. I found the nearest grocery store and started feeding everyone.

Doug smiled and didn't complain when I had him eat at his dining room table and talk to me, instead of just scarfing down crap while sitting in front of the TV and staring at whatever junk was on while he ate his junk food.

"So, what's the deal with your sister?" I asked eventually, knowing she was his only living relative, but they weren't close, especially lately. I knew Doug needed more help—I'd seen mail piled up in stacks, unopened—but I was just a friend.

"I don't talk to her anymore." His face looked very serious. I felt bad asking. I liked Doug's smile. It could light up a whole room. Now he stared down at the chicken and steamed vegetables I'd made for him.

"You mean, because of what happened with your parents?" I was guessing.

"That didn't help."

When he didn't say anything else, I put my hand on his and leaned in closer. "We don't have to talk about that. I just wondered how you were ... handling everything." I glanced at the piles of bills.

"As far as I'm concerned, she's not my sister anymore."

"I'm sorry to hear that, sweetie."

"That's okay, I'm happy for you. You're lucky to have each other." He hesitated a moment. "But since you mentioned handling things ..." He trailed off and looked in the direction of the stack of mail. "I can't really read all that fine print anymore."

"I saw some bills and stuff over there, can I help you with those?"

He exhaled. "That would be great."

I learned Doug had been paying someone to do some shopping. But the housework like dusting was not going well, and while he was good at keeping up his finances in general, that started to get more difficult with his vision loss. Eventually, I helped him with writing checks for his various bills. "Maybe I should let this cable bill slide," I joked with him. "You watch too much TV anyway. That shit'll make you go blind."

"Oops, oh well," he smiled, and I was glad he didn't mind my humor. He liked to listen to the news and some history channel shows and Jeopardy while we sat there on his recliner. He had so much random trivia in his head.

One day there was a category on real estate terms, and he knew every single one, and never forgot to say the answer as a question, like "What is escrow?" When it was over, Doug asked me, "What happened to that condo you had right off the Ala Wai? Did you rent it out?"

That would've been smart. But that's not what happened.

"No, the bank took it back," I said, missing the place.

"Shoot. That's too bad. Can you negotiate with them?"

"Nope. Done deal. The money I used to pay for that was from bad stuff, anyway. So, you're stuck with ME helping YOU with your bills. You might be in trouble."

He turned off the TV, held my hand, and looked right at me. I knew he could see me.

"Mary, honey, there's no one in the world I'd rather have helping me right now. These last couple of weeks since you've been here," he got a little choked up, "so much fun. I don't even mind that you're feeding all the cats in Vegas on my patio."

I laughed. Didn't know if he knew how many cats were actually out there, telling all their feral friends to come over for the free buffet.

"Or, maybe I should say, YOUR patio." He paused for a second before going on. "I want you to have this place when I'm gone, It's all paid off."

"Doug! But what about your..."

"Sister? No. I got no family. You're my only family."

I gave him an awkward sideways hug there on the recliner. Tears filled my eyes. "I don't want to think about when you're gone, you're doing better now, eating better and everything."

"Yes, thanks to Auntie 'Ria's cooking." He teased me about my name. I'd been Mary to him as long as he'd known me. After I got out of the life and started going to church again, I called myself Mary more and more. But here in Vegas, where I'd reconnected with some other old friends who still lived here or had moved here, sometimes I went by Maria again. One of the girls I knew, a friend of a friend who needed someone to watch her little one, called me "Auntie 'Ria" and it stuck.

Sitting next to Doug, in this town I hated so much, with the illness I wished hadn't taken my friend's sight, I glanced out at the patio... our patio... where more cats had come for dinner. God had sent me here, to look after Doug, to make him laugh, for however much time he had left in this life. And to feed all the hungry kitties.

I turned to Doug, who looked so content, and touched his cheek. "You know I love you, right, Dougie?"

He smiled and nodded.

"And not just 'cuz you're giving me your condo."

He laughed.

Chapter Thirty-Three

Found

"About you leaving me your condo," I began, still not sure how all this would work. Sometimes we got on each other's nerves as we adjusted to living together. Mentally we seemed to be getting better with each other's company, most days. But physically, we were both falling apart.

"Yes?"

"We don't know for sure that I'm going to outlive you. I'm no spring chicken anymore, look at this knee. Can you feel it?" I put his hand on my swollen knee, which was barely taking me up the stairs to the loft where I'd moved all my stuff.

"You got two of those. I only have one ticker," he joked.

"That's true. You win."

"I lose," he said. "But I have you, so I win."

"Aww, you're too sweet."

I touched his cheek, so happy he still had his sense of humor and his kindness, despite everything else that wasn't working well for him. He didn't need to worry about what if something happened to me, even though I did.

As though reading my thoughts, he said, "If you go first, I now have all these kitties to take care of me."

A few days later, he heard me cursing as I tried to get up the stairs on my bum knee. "Mary, why are you doing that to yourself? You can stay down here."

I hobbled over to sit next to him.

"You're right, I can sleep here on the recliner."

He picked up my hand and squeezed it. "Don't be silly, We'll trade rooms."

"You don't have to—"

He squeezed my hand again. "I don't have to do anything. But I want to."

"Thank you, Dougie. You know you're the kindest man."

"I'm wondering... I want to ask you something."

"Anything at all, Dougie."

He hesitated a moment longer, and my worry kicked into high gear.

"Will you marry me?" He smiled and his eyes twinkled. "No funny stuff. But we love each other and take care of each other."

My mouth dropped open. I hadn't expected him to say that.

"And I have better health insurance than you."

I started to laugh. So did he.

"And we make each other laugh!" I added.

"We do." He let out a long breath, and I realized I hadn't given him an answer.

"And I do." I smiled.

"You do? Like, you'll marry me? I could get down on one knee." He moved closer to the edge of his seat.

"You know neither one of us should be getting down on any knees."

He gently touched my leg. "A good reason why we should get hitched sooner rather than later. No need for you to be in pain. Tricare has all kinds of orthopedists."

I thought of how happy Delilah would be about us getting married. She'd wanted me to be with Doug since she was a girl, and now she had her own girl, who'd gain a grandpa! Would she want to be a flower girl? Tears started to come. I held them back. I couldn't imagine having an actual wedding with other people.

"Also," Doug seemed to think I needed more convincing, even though I'd already agreed, "you'll still have Tricare after I'm gone."

His words, after I'm gone caused the tears to flood out. I covered my eyes and let out a sob, my forehead on his shoulder.

"Shhh, shhh, it's okay," he stroked my hair. "I didn't mean to make you cry."

I pulled myself together, wiping the tears from my eyes.

"I'm just so happy, Doug." This was true. "My whole life, since ... forever," I wasn't going to say Marvin's name out loud at that moment, "I've picked the wrong men to love."

He nodded, listening.

"I didn't even know what real love meant." Nothing to do with sex or looks or where you come from or what you do for a living.

He stroked my hair again and squeezed my hand.

"Now God has sent me you, Dougie. I guess He sent me you a very long time ago, but I was too dumb to figure it out."

It was Doug's turn to get a little teary-eyed. "Hey, don't call my fiancée dumb. You are so smart, and look how you set up your Auntie Ria's business so fast. I still remember how you sold those Japanese language tapes."

The memory of those tapes I recorded made me giggle. They were to teach the other girls working in Waikiki enough Japanese to have a conversation with the tourists, way before smartphones or apps. I sold them for hundreds of dollars to lots of the girls, even separate copies to two sisters who were fighting. And I'd grown my Auntie Ria's childcare business here in Vegas in record time, thanks to social media and old-fashioned word-of-mouth.

Doug knew the real me, all of it. He appreciated what I could do and didn't care about what I wasn't so great at. He loved me more than I loved myself. And I loved him more than he loved himself. Maybe that's why God put couples together, so we could lift each other up.

He held both my hands. "We can get you a ring if you want. I know how you like jewelry."

Throughout the decades there had been much wealthier men I could have married—and so much jewelry from them and pieces I'd bought myself. Some of the offers of marriage came from rich guys who were polite and handsome. Could've gone the Pretty Woman route, like a lot of girls did. But my heart was not for sale. Doug and I had something much more intimate than sex or anything physical. We knew each other through-and-through.

We even started to look like each other, wearing similar colors by accident, as if our brains were in sync.

Without telling anyone—either one of us could have a medical issue and have to reschedule—we planned a tiny, just-us wedding. All the way up to the day we got married, I kept saying to Doug, "You don't have to do this."

He smiled. "Nothing else I'd rather do."

I knew he'd picked out his best dark-blue pants, a sky-blue shirt and a peach sweater to tie around his neck—he always loved the 80s. I chose a peach blouse and blue skirt, with simple flats that wouldn't hurt my bad knees and some cat fur for flair.

We'd gone to a local jewelry store for rings, since he knew I liked a little bling, even if my tastes had gotten much more down-to-earth recently. God's beauty. I put on just a touch of makeup, the first time since I'd officially joined the church and left the life. When Doug stepped out of his bathroom, all dressed and ready, I took a deep breath and noticed something else different.

"You even put on your smell good!"

He smiled and giggled.

"You clean up nice," I said.

"So do you." He touched my cheek.

We both giggled. We were giddy, like a couple of teenagers getting ready to elope in Vegas.

My car wasn't working at the time, so we had to catch an Uber to the courthouse. We filled out all the paperwork to make it legal, then went across the street to an adorable little chapel, to have our marriage blessed by God. We giggled the whole way.

"If you ever have any second thoughts, my sweet Dougie, it's not too late to get this annulled."

"No way," he said. "I'm telling everyone. We need to make copies of the paperwork. Last stop, Kinkos."

I wasn't sure if he was serious about Kinkos, but I knew he was serious about me. We'd gotten into the habit of telling each other my favorite last words of the day, like I'd said to my sister since forever, "Goodnight, God bless you, I love you."

It took us a while to cross the street to the chapel. I'd learned how to walk with a blind man and his walker. He'd taught me something even more important—patience. My whole life I'd been in a hurry to get onto the next next thing, next customer, next chapter of my life. The next baby to change in a daycare where they only gave you so many seconds to change a diaper and move onto another baby. Here in these moments with Doug—precious minutes we both knew could be some of his last—I learned to breathe in his smell-good, enjoy the sounds of his laugh, and be grateful God had brought me this kind man, decades ago, before I had the wisdom to see this gift right in front of me.

At the tiny chapel, a cute, older couple did everything -- the music, the vows, the photos. You could tell they loved doing it.

"Do you take this woman," the nice man asked, "to be your lawfully wedded wife?"

"I do," he said, adding, "I love you so much, Mary."

"I love you, too, Doug," I kissed him on the cheek.

We'd gone off script. Written our own. The chaplain caught up.

"Uh, you may now kiss the bride?"

Doug kissed me once more. He giggled again. Me too. Crazy giddy. He touched my back, and turned to face his walker and the door. "So next stop Kinkos?"

"You weren't kidding?"

"Nope, I wanna make sure we tell everyone, now that it's official!" I'd never heard him so insistent or excited.

"Okay then."

The wife handed me a beautiful certificate before we headed out the door. I described it to Doug.

"Copies of that, too. Mahalo."

I thought Doug might start skipping. I wanted to skip, too, at the sight of his huge, beaming smile.

"You have the best smile," I patted his pink cheek.

"I feel like my face is gonna explode from grinning so big."

I felt like my heart might explode from his love. And God's love. But I didn't want to talk about any exploding body parts. Too close to the truth.

"Me too," I said instead. "I'm so happy to be your wife, and I'm cookin' you a nice dinner when we get home."

"That sounds great, Mrs. Mau." He was especially thrilled that I'd be changing my name. "Right after we stop at Kinkos."

The young woman who made the copies called us, "the most adorable couple I've ever seen." She added, "And I've seen way more than my fair share of newlyweds."

For dinner, I made Doug's favorite, Buffalo wings. None of that frozen crap he'd been eating before I showed up. As a girl from Buffalo, I knew how to make them for real, from scratch. Just the right amount of spice. Some potato salad to take the edge off the spice. And applesauce, because that was my favorite. We sat down in our usual spots for dinner, which was simple, real, not too spicy. Like our love for each other.

After dinner we watched a little TV and held hands. I knew we'd be together—as long as we both shall live—however long we had.

Before we went to sleep, he kissed me on the cheek again, and we told each other, "Goodnight, God bless you, I love you."

I never slept so well in my life.

Photos

Mary as an infant

Marvin and Mary

Mary's first wedding

Mary, pre-surgeries

TRICKED

Baby D and Mary

Mary and grandbaby

Biggest wedding

Mary on her Jag

Mary with the babes

Mary and Eddie

Miracle Mary on a mission

Doug and Mary

Epilogue

One Year Later

Epilogue: One Year Later

I'm so grateful God brought me to Doug for the final chapter of his life. When I first arrived, Doug's condo was too still, with dust and sadness piled high. He wasn't sure about all the cats I kept feeding and taming, but eventually he had two favorite kitties of his own that kept him company. The human babies and little ones I brought home as part of my Auntie Ria's daycare made him laugh and get plenty of hugs and love all the time. I'd never seen him smile or laugh so much.

The final weeks of Doug's life involved some difficult medical challenges, which I believe were less scary with me by his side, and Delilah when she could.

During the final moments of his life, he whispered his last words to me, "I love you." He smiled, closed his eyes, slowly stopped breathing, and joined God.

I can still feel him here in his place. In my heart. He'll be with me forever, making me smile, feel beautiful and strong. Giving me the confidence to love myself and all those around me, both two-legged and furry four-legged. Cheering me on as I write the next chapter of my story, wherever it may lead.

Acknowledgements

From Mary Mau:
I thank God every day for the blessings He has given me, saving me in so many different ways, when I would have given up on myself.

Although my mother was not there for me very long, and she did give up on herself, her weaknesses in a way made me stronger, and inspired me to persevere where she did not. Also, she brought me my dear Nana who has made a huge difference in my life and so much love. Inspiring me to love others the way she always loved me, even through her own struggles.

The people who have helped me over the years (many who appear in this book, with their names changed for privacy) could fill volumes. I will mention some here, by first name only, also for privacy: Rene, Sharon, Sherly, Merle, Mary, Nicky, Chris (and the whole gang at Made in Hope), and all my friends at First Presbyterian and Blue Water Mission in Hawaii. Also huge thanks to Dr. George & SJ for helping me find my way to sanity.

My big sister and brother--I'm so grateful to you, and can't wait to spend our next chapters together.

Delilah: you gave me reason to be a better person, and to keep trying to be a better person over and over even though I made mistakes and will continue to make mistakes. I will always love you, more than you can know.

My beautiful granddaughter amazes and inspires, I love you so much!

Goodnight, God bless you, and I love you.

From Mary StJohn-Putnam:

So many people have helped with this book that I'll likely forget to list some. Please forgive. Also know that any errors, typos, I did my best to catch but I know I've missed some in spite of the help from so many people. I hope you'll reach out with feedback so I can correct as many as possible in future updates.

Big thanks to Lisa Daily for her professional writing coach help--which I'd recommend to any and all trying to finish and publish a book. I can't thank you enough for your infinite patience, help on so many fronts, and friendship.

Like a couple of multi-talented and super-supportive big sisters: K-B Gressitt and Judy Bernstein have spent countless hours helping me with getting words on the page in a much better way than my not-so-great first drafts, and for soooo much moral support when I felt as though I wasn't up to the task. I could not have done it without you.

I'm super grateful to my Honolulu, Del Luz, and Asilomar writers' groups. You're all rock stars and like family to me.

Marie Iding, my awesome mentor and friend, thank you for all your help both craft-wise and on the staying-sane front. Muchos mahalos and aloha.

Carol Patterson gave us a much-needed shot in the arm (during COVID lock-down no less) as Mary and I worked to revamp and reboot our book-writing efforts. Thank you for all your love and friendship, and excellent questions. I am so glad you narrowly escaped your brush with getting snatched/trafficked in Vegas.

Also thanks to Jean Femia, Stacey Enersen, Mary Webb, and my Calix buddies especially Jeannine, Arizona, and Tonya.

When I met my beloved mega-talented husband, David Putnam, in a writers' workshop 30 years ago, I had no idea the many joys he would bring into my life. One of the greatest so far is the phenomenal and inspiring Mary Mau.

Mary, I'm so honored and humbled that you trusted me with your incredible story, friendship, and love. I'm grateful for your infinite patience with me as I stumbled and struggled to do justice to your story in a not-so-timely manner, with so many fits and starts. I can't wait to see where the next chapters lead, how you will continue to grow, inspire, and bring light to others all around the world. You're truly a blessing, and I'm so glad to call you friend.

Last thoughts

Mary's Mau's next chapter(s) involve leaving Las Vegas (yay!). She's sold Doug's condo and will be hitting the road, moving across the country to live near her brother and big sister again in New York.

We're also setting up book tour stops starting in Hawaii. We love speaking to groups both large and small. Please reach out to us via our websites:

Mary Mau: www.MaryMau.com
Writer Mary: www.BitofMary.com

Aloha and Mahalo!
Mary & Mary